Bible Humor top

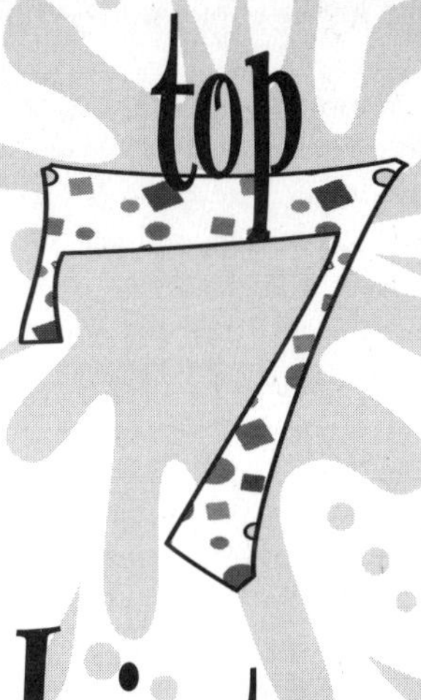

Lists

Rich Anderson and Dave Veerman

WORD PUBLISHING
NASHVILLE
A Thomas Nelson Company

Produced with the assistance of The Livingstone Corporation—Alan Sharrer and Dave Veerman, project staff, with contributions from Bruce Barton, Todd Bernheardt Jon Farrar, James Galvin, Chris Hudson, Linda Taylor, Bruce Watkins, Neil Wilson, and Len Woods.

ISBN 0-7394-0740-6

Printed in the United States of America

Acknowledgments

Rich Anderson thanks Bruce Watkins and St. Bernie, the patron saint of humor, for their creative input and outrageous sense of humor. He also thanks his wife, Kristin, for her great laugh even when it's the fourth time around for the same punch line. Rich dedicates this book to Elsie Smith, whose childhood stories helped spark the creativity in a young boy—now all grown up.

Dave Veerman thanks his partners, Bruce Barton and Jim Galvin, compatriots in business and in humor. We sure laugh a lot at Livingstone!

Introduction

Those born and reared in Christian homes usually have a very serious view of Scripture. That is to say, we view the message and character of biblical people like Moses, Noah, Solomon, the apostle Paul, and especially prophets like Elijah and Elisha very seriously.

For example, try picturing Elijah telling Elisha knock-knock jokes . . . or Paul sharing a humorous anecdote in a letter to the Romans or Corinthians. Imagine reading, "Come unto me all ye that labor and are heavy laden, and I will telleth you a joke!" or "Study to show thyself approved unto God, a workman of great humor."

You will have a difficult time finding the word "humor" in your Bible. (I looked real hard to no avail.) So why a book of Bible humor? Because I, for one, think that guys like Paul and the disciples enjoyed laughter. They had a sense of humor created by God for their enjoyment as well as for his.

Imagine the laughter from Simon, James, and John as they recounted the incredible fishing experience they had with Jesus after fishing the same waters all night without success. Or how about the stories around the campfire about the look on the pigs' faces after Jesus had sent the demons into them at Gadara. Perhaps that's where the phrase "when pigs fly" was coined!

Proverbs 17:22 reminds us that, "A cheerful heart is good medicine, but a broken spirit saps a person's strength" (NLT). My hope is that this book will be good medicine for your spirit. As Dave and I have written and edited this book, we've included a variety of humor styles, everything from "groaner" puns to more cerebral biblical references. And at times you will find a serious lesson behind the joke. We pray that God will bless you, cheer you, and strengthen you as you read!

By the way, this book will also be a valuable resource for pastors, teachers, and youth leaders. Think of the response from your congregation or class when you drop in a little-known fact like the shortest man in the Bible or a Top 7 list.

In his grip,

Rich Anderson

The Old Testament

How do we know that Adam could run fast?

Answer

He was first in the human race.

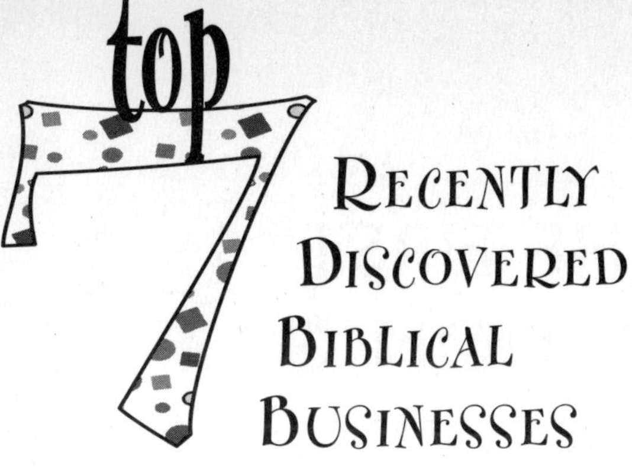

Top 7 Recently Discovered Biblical Businesses

7 Eve's Forbidden Fruits and Vegetables—"One bite will change your world."

6 Egyptian Chariot Company—"All chariots warranted for seven years or one hundred days' journey. Void if submerged in salt water."

5 Saul's Spears 'R' Us—"Try our fine selection of battle and leisure spears."

4 The Pilate Soap Company—"Specializing in decorative soft soap dispensers (does not include guilt, shame, or sin—some restrictions apply)."

3 Paul's Lighting Emporium—"From tamper-proof prison lights to blinding lights, you'll find it at Paul's."

2 McHades—"Billions and billions burned."

1 Salvation, Inc.—"Never hunger, never thirst, never die. Salvation, Inc. That's salvation in Christ."

THE FIRST MENTION OF FREEWAYS

The Lord made every "creeping thing."

Genesis 1:24, KJV

Top 7 Complaints of Eve in the Garden

7 Adam never takes her anywhere.

6 She had girl names all picked out but got stuck with boys.

5 There's nothing good on television since *Garden Improvement* ended.

4 She never has a thing to wear.

3 Adam leaves the lid up.

2 How are you supposed to keep up with the Joneses when there are no Joneses?

1 When Adam calls her his little "Riblet."

Who is the first man in the Bible?

Answer

"Chap." 1.

Top 7 Reasons That God Created Eve

7 God worried that Adam would get lost in the Garden and refuse to ask for directions.

6 How else was Adam to remember which night was garbage night?

5 God knew that if the world was to be populated, men would never be able to handle childbearing.

4 As keeper of the Garden, Adam would likely forget where he put his tools.

3 Beans and Spaghettio's would have gotten really old, and TV dinners weren't invented yet.

2 Proverbs 31 was predestined to be written.

1 Adam needed another tax deduction.

How did Adam and Eve feel when expelled from the Garden of Eden?

Answer

They were really put out.

LACONIC LIMERICK #1

Genesis 4:2–12

There once were two sons at the table
who wanted the favorite label.
But missing the mark,
Cain struck in the dark,
knowing he just wasn't Abel.

How did Adam and Eve react when they were kicked out of the Garden?

Answer

They raised Cain.

Old Testament Vanity Plates

7 FRST M8—Eve

6 RED 1—Esau

5 PEGGY—Jael (Judges 4:21)

4 I B KNG 2—Rehoboam

3 X LEPR—Naaman

2 WALZ—Nehemiah

1 4 TELL—Ezekiel

What excuse did Adam give to his children as to why he no longer lived in Eden?

Answer

Your mother ate us out of house and home.

Top 7 Recently Discovered Quotes from Famous Biblical Dads

7 Adam (to Cain and Abel)—"You guys got dates? Where did you find girls?"

6 Noah—"What do you mean we're out of Dramamine?"

5 Abraham (in thick Jewish accent)—"Slow down, Isaac. I'm not one hundred anymore!"

4 Jesse (to David)—"One of these days you're gonna hit somebody right in the head with that slingshot of yours!"

3 King Saul (to David)—"Who died and made you king?"

2 David (to Absalom)—"As long as you're living under my roof, no son of mine is gonna have long hair like that!"

1 Solomon—"Why is it I can solve the world's problems but I can't figure out my teenagers?"

Who was the oldest man who ever lived and yet died before his father?

Answer

Methuselah, who lived to be 969; his father, Enoch, never died because "God took him."

(Genesis 5:18–27)

Top 7 Pet Peeves of Noah

7 Sons Shem, Ham, and Japheth would always hog the deck chairs.

6 He ran out of air fresheners around Day 27.

5 It's not a "boat" . . . it's an "ark."

4 Constantly having to explain that "gopher wood" and the *Love Boat* character are unrelated.

3 Direct TV hadn't been invented yet.

2 His insurance expired the day before the crash landing on Mount Ararat.

1 Eight people, one bathroom.

Why was there no card-playing on the ark?

Answer

Because Noah sat on the deck.

Top 7 Rejected Names for Noah's Ark

7 The Gopher Wood Tub o' Fun

6 The Party-Buster Barge

5 Mrs. Noah's Toy

4 The Floating Zoo in a Box

3 The Gospel Ship

2 The Floodmobile

1 Captain Noah's Second Mortgage

Where did Noah keep his bees?

Answer

In the archives ("ark hives").

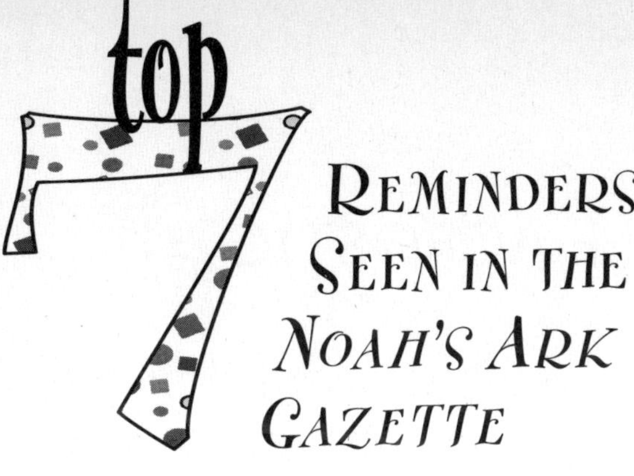

top 7 Reminders Seen in the *Noah's Ark Gazette*

7 No more comedy shows in the hyena pen.

6 The termite couple is no longer allowed on the lower deck.

5 The next person to start the "Old MacDonald" song swims the rest of the way.

4 Please do feed the animals.

3 If you shower last, please remember to close the sunroof.

2 When we finally arrive, try not to forget where we park.

1 No hunting!

BIBLE ACROSTIC #1

Noah could have called his operation SURF:

Sudden

Urge to

Rescue the

Family

Top 7 Complaints About Bible Wives

7 Sarah—She never takes Abraham seriously.

6 Mrs. Lot—She's always overseasoning his food.

5 Mrs. Noah—She's a backseat driver.

4 Jael—She misuses her husband's tools. (Judges 5:26).

3 Zipporah—She nags Moses about throwing his staff down in the dining room.

2 Mrs. Job—She's always making foolish remarks.

1 Solomon's wives—They leave all those pantyhose in the bathroom.

Who was the greatest financier in the Bible?

Answer

Noah—he was floating his stock while everyone else was in liquidation.

Top 7 Favorite Christmas Gifts of Select Bible Characters

7 From the disciples, Peter received a pet rock and Popeil's Pocket Fisher-o'-men.

6 Ham and Japeth gave Noah male and female Chia Pets.

5 In order to imitate Esau better, Jacob requested "spray-on hair" and Rogaine.

4 David requested a self-cleaning, repeating slingshot.

3 Gideon received a Bible and then promptly left it in his hotel room.

2 Peter was given a Paul and Mary CD.

1 The church at Corinth received a pocket translator for tongues.

What kind of lights did Noah have on the ark?

Answer

Floodlights.

Top 7 Instructions Not Recorded in Scripture

7 How to properly execute a foot wash

6 How to legally tell the truth while lying

5 How to get ahead when fighting a giant

4 Baking hints when in a fiery furnace

3 How to conduct waste management on the ark

2 Where to put mountains when you move them

1 Proper skin care when stuck in the belly of a great fish

What do you call the study of the Ark?

Answer

Ark-eology.

top 7 Reasons Lot's Wife Turned When Leaving Sodom

7 She thought she left the iron on.

6 The kids double-dared her.

5 She thought the angels had said "pillar of the community."

4 She thought it was a sure way to become a spokesperson for Morton International, Inc.

3 She thought Lot was lost and wanted to ask for directions.

2 She forgot to use the bathroom before leaving.

1 She didn't want to miss the Wal-Mart of Sodom's twelve-hour sale.

LACONIC LIMERICK #2

Genesis 19:26

Lot's wife had one tiny fault,
Though God had told her to halt,
despite what he said,
she still turned her head,
and the trespass became an assault.

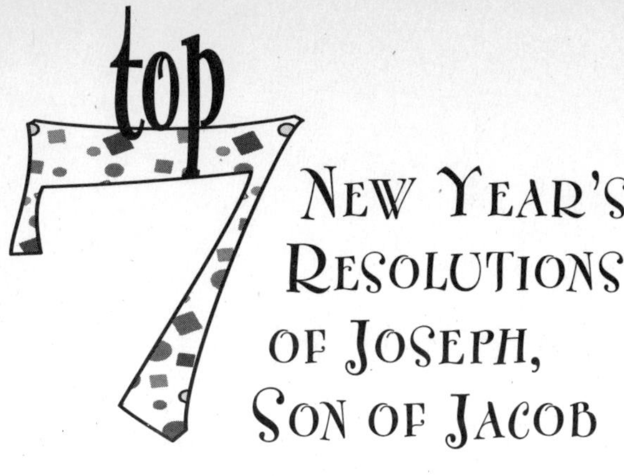

New Year's Resolutions of Joseph, Son of Jacob

7 Get pants of many colors to go with the coat.

6 Get rid of the T-shirt that says "I'm Dad's Favorite."

5 Don't fall for the old "we've got a really neat pit to show you" trick.

4 Never listen to the boss's wife.

3 Write a Broadway musical.

2 Ratify NAEFTA (the North African–Egyptian Free Trade Agreement).

1 Once and for all, interpret that "falling" dream.

Where is smoking mentioned in the Bible?

Answer

"And Rebekah lifted up her eyes, and when she saw Isaac, she lighted off the camel."

(Genesis 24:64, KJV)

Biblical Fitness Videos

7 *Geriatric Workout*—Methuselah shows how to shave two to three hundred off your figure.

6 *Noah's Pecs of Steel*—Chop enough gopher wood to build your own ark.

5 Moses' *Forty-Year Walk to Better Health*

4 Joshua's *Aerobic Marching* (do not try this at home)

3 *You Too Can Be a Lean, Mean, Killing Machine*, with Samson (includes free jawbone)

2 *Run for Your Life*, with Elijah (crazy woman and chariot not included)

1 Daniel's *Veggie Trails* for health, fitness, and bureaucratic fast-trackers

MR. COOL?

"And Jacob said . . . I am a smooth man."

(Genesis 27:11, KJV)

New Year's Resolutions of Moses

7 Steer clear of combustible shrubbery.

6 Learn to dress more like Charlton Heston.

5 Do not do the leprous hand trick at the dinner table.

4 Brush up on palace "knock-knock" jokes to humor Pharaoh.

3 For future close encounters with God, stock up on that "no shine" face powder.

2 Call AAA before the next trip.

1 Read *How to Win Friends and Influence Two Million Israelites.*

Who was the greatest female financier in the Bible?

Answer

Pharaoh's daughter—she went down to the bank of the Nile and drew out a little prophet (profit).

Top 7 Standby Plagues Not Inflicted on Egypt

7 Cause all secondborn males to be picked last for kickball teams

6 Cause an infestation of nose-hair lice

5 Turn the Nile River into salsa and hide all the tortilla chips

4 Cause the land to be overrun by millions of ravenous wild toy poodles

3 Threaten not to cast Yul Brenner in *The Ten Commandments*

2 Change all palace singers into Barry Manilow soundalikes

1 Turn all pyramids into Berry Blue Jell-O Jigglers

BIBLE ACROSTIC #2

Moses could have called the wilderness expedition SAND:

Strategic
Advance to
New
Destination

or SPUDS:

Special
People
Urging
Deliverance from
Slavery

Top 7 Pet Peeves of Pharoah

7 He had to wear a dunce cap in school 'cause he never got what people told him.

6 His weekend cruise down the Nile was ruined.

5 Those dang plagues.

4 He couldn't beat Moses at thumb wrestling.

3 Moses and Aaron didn't take off their sandals at the door.

2 He had to buy new recruiting posters after the Red Sea expedition.

1 After Israel left, he couldn't find a decent bagel anywhere.

Why was Moses the most wicked person in the Bible?

Answer

He broke all the commandments at the same time. (Exodus 32:19)

Top 7 Commandments That Weren't

7 Thou shalt not listen to country music.

6 Thou shalt obey the speed limit at all times.

5 Thou shalt not have a communion service on Super Bowl Sunday.

4 Dabble not in the lottery but supporteth church bingo.

3 Seeketh not what the mall has to offer.

2 Let not your prayers exceedeth the length of the "Hallelujah Chorus" during church-related functions.

1 Thou shalt useth onlyeth the Kingeth Jameseth Bibleth.

GOOD NEWS FOR DIETERS

"All the fat is the Lord's."

(Leviticus 3:16b)

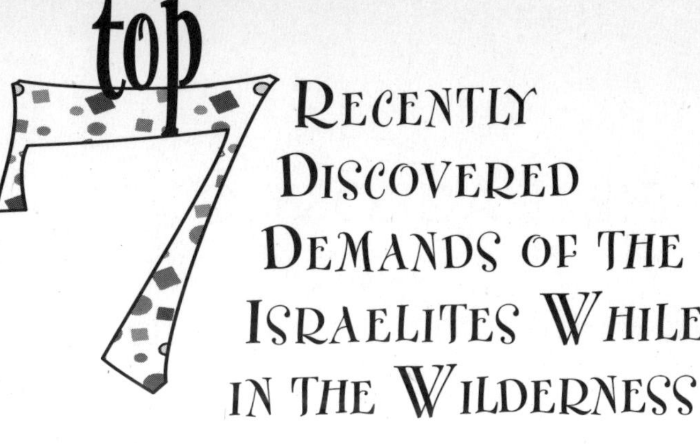

top 7 Recently Discovered Demands of the Israelites While in the Wilderness

7 Air-conditioned tents with skylights

6 Waveless water cots

5 Plastic sand toys

4 Sunscreen and taffeta beach towels

3 A look at the map and navigator's notes

2 A dry path back across the Red Sea

1 Miracle Whip (a manna sandwich just isn't complete without Miracle Whip)

BIBLE ACROSTIC #3

The Levites could have identified their tribe by PANTS:

People

Associated for

New

Tabernacle

Sacrifices

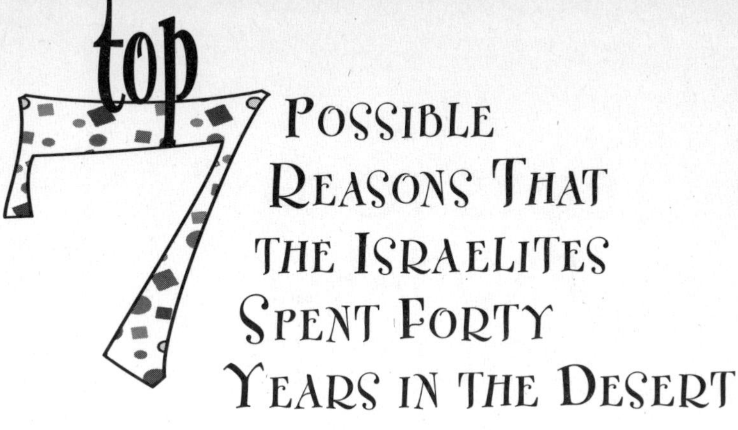

Possible Reasons That the Israelites Spent Forty Years in the Desert

7 They needed more frequent chariot mileage.

6 The map was written in hieroglyphics, and they had it upside down.

5 They kept stopping to take pictures.

4 They became hooked on manna.

3 They took a wrong turn at Rephidim.

2 The kids kept asking, "Are we there yet?"

1 They didn't have exact change at the wilderness tollbooth.

BOYS TODAY PROBABLY WOULDN'T GO FOR THIS

"And Moses brought Aaron's sons, and put coats upon them, and girded them with girdles, and put bonnets upon them."

(Leviticus 8:13, KJV)

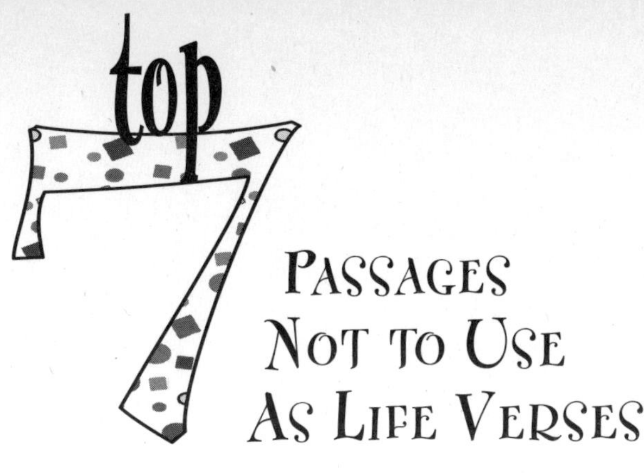

Top 7 Passages Not to Use as Life Verses

7 Job 2:9, NLT—"Curse God and die."

6 Luke 18:4, NLT—"I fear neither God nor man."

5 Luke 12:20, NLT—"You fool! You will die this very night. Then who will get it all?"

4 Lamentations 4:8—"Their skin has shriveled on their bones; it has become as dry as a stick."

3 Leviticus 3:10, NLT—"both kidneys with the fat on them near the loins, and the covering of the liver, which he will remove with the kidneys."

2 Judges 16:13—"Until now, you have been making a fool of me and lying to me."

1 Proverbs 23:8, KJV—"The morsel which thou hast eaten shalt thou vomit up, and lose thy sweet words."

PET CENTRAL

"And the ferret, and the chameleon, and the lizard, and the snail, and the mole."

(Leviticus 11:30, KJV)

Top 7 Pick-Up Lines of the Children of Israel in the Wilderness

7 Dost thou come here often?

6 I wouldst invite thee on the town if we had a town.

5 My, but that is a lovely, shapeless, drab robe you've been wearing all year.

4 Oh yes, Moses and I areth good chums. Wouldst thou like to meet him?

3 Didst thou know that Manna Breath Mints lasteth a long season?

2 We areth not related, art we?

1 Canst I interest thou in a Gaithers concert? I hearest they art having a reunion.

FIRST MENTION OF CREDIT CARDS

"And Moses charged the people the same day."

(Deuteronomy 27:11, KJV)

Uses for Manna Not Recorded in Scripture

7 Manna crumb trails to figure out once and for all if they're going in circles

6 Manna-boarding in the wilderness foothills

5 Practical joke—to smell up a place, hide an omer of manna in someone's tent (Exodus 16:16–20)

4 Predating the popular "I love you, man": "I love you, manna!"

3 Bamanna splits, mannanaise, and Mannachevitz

2 New position in government for the manna overseer—"mannager"

1 The ultimate food fight—"manna-war"

Where is basketball mentioned in the Bible?

Answer

"Blessed shall be your basket."

(Deuteronomy 28:5, NKJV)

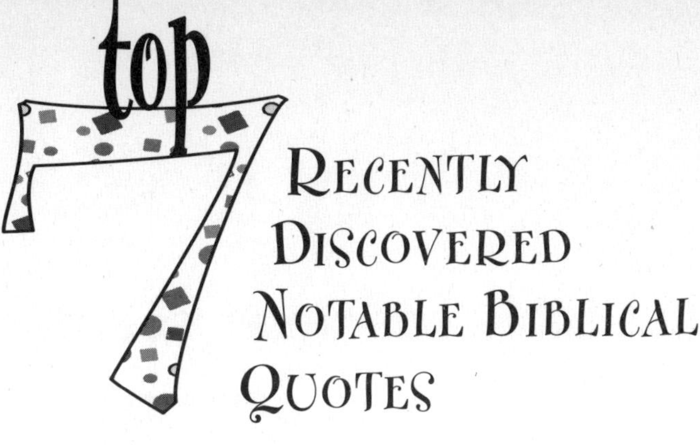

Recently Discovered Notable Biblical Quotes

7 Eve when disciplining Cain and Abel—"Now when I was your age . . . wait a minute, I never was your age!"

6 Noah when asked what an "ark" was—"It's kinda like a breadbox, only bigger."

5 Methuselah after outliving all his friends—"Happy Birthday to me, Happy Birthday to me . . ."

4 "You want it when?"—Bezalel (Exodus 36)

3 Pharaoh to Moses—"Speak to the hand."

2 "I'm beside myself."—Malchus (John 18:10)

1 Satan's favorite—"Behold, I stand at the door and pick the lock."

What Bible character seems to have had no parents?

Answer

Joshua—he was the son of Nun ("none").

Top 7 Alternate Plans for Conquering Jericho

7 Play disco music all day, all the time.

6 Offer lox and bagels to all who surrender.

5 Invite all citizens to an Amway party at Rahab's house.

4 Give everyone's number to a telemarketing company.

3 Lob saber-toothed locusts over the walls.

2 Read Chronicles through a ram's horn.

1 Use five smooth boulders and a really big slingshot.

LACONIC LIMERICK #3

Joshua 7:4–8:26

Ai was theirs for the takin',
but the army God had forsaken,
So though favored, they lost
and counted the cost
The cause of it all, he was Achan.

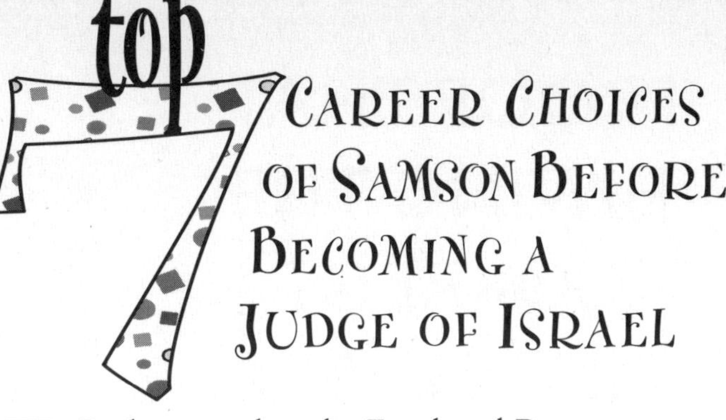

Top 7 Career Choices of Samson Before Becoming a Judge of Israel

7 Beekeeper—but the Food and Drug Administration felt that using lion carcasses as beehives did not meet federal standards.

6 Church deacon—but the leaders within the church found his long hair to be worldly and offensive.

5 Animal rights activist—but a small scandal erupted when it was discovered that he had attached torches to fox tails.

4 Luggage manufacturer—but decided "Samsonite" was a name that would never go well with luggage.

3 Used-chariot salesman—but a major recall by the Ezekiel Tire and Wheel Corporation left chariot sales flat.

2 Tag-team wrestler—but everybody refused to get in the ring with him because he wouldn't fake any of the action.

1 Marriage counselor—but after a couple of his own marriages failed, he decided a new career was in order.

PROOF THAT HAVING THE CORRECT TIME IS VERY IMPORTANT

"They had but newly set the watch."

(Judges 7:19, KJV)

"The young man that kept the watch."

(2 Samuel 13:34, KJV)

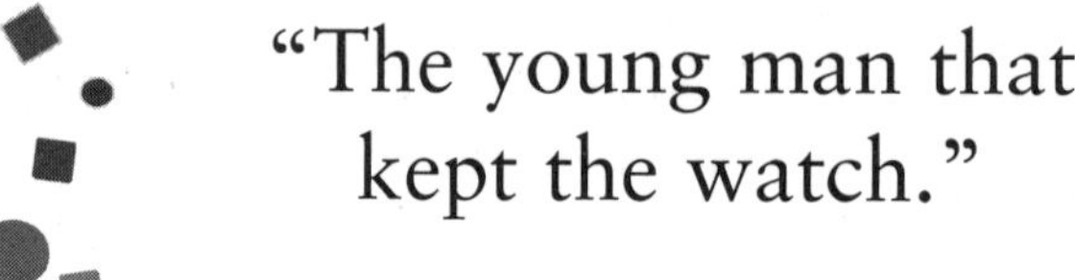

Potluck Dishes of Bible Characters

7 Eve's forbidden-fruit salad

6 Moses' quail-a-bobs

5 Manoah's wife's nonfruit punch

4 Elijah's Cajun blackened sacrifice

3 John the Baptist's locusts-and-wild-honey casserole

2 The disciples' bottomless basket-o'-fish sandwich

1 John's baked sweet scrolls (Revelation 10:9–11)

BONUS: Samson's carcass-dipped honey bars (Judges 14:5–9)

BIBLE ACROSTIC #4

Gideon could have challenged the men of Israel to join his contingent of JARS:

Judgment
Against
Religious
Syncretism

Why is Samson known as a great entertainer?

Answer

He brought the whole house down!

(Judges 16:29–30)

Top 7 Facts Samson Doesn't Want You to Know About Him

7 He cries at weddings.

6 He can't stand that "fingernails on the blackboard" sound.

5 He fantasizes about being part of the World Wrestling Federation.

4 He wants to be the thirteenth judge of Israel because he likes the way he looks in those judicial robes.

3 Sure, he can rip the gates off a city wall, but those goofy Chinese finger traps get him every time.

2 He isn't a real blond.

1 Delilah's nickname for him is "Binkie-pooh."

LACONIC LIMERICK #4

Ruth 1:8–3:4

Naomi asked Ruth not to go as
    a widow, but Ruth went there so as
        together their plan
        was to find Ruth a man.
Let's just hope all boys will be Boaz.

top 7 Campaign Slogans for Famous Biblical Leaders

7 Pharaoh—"Endorsed by *Better Pyramids and Gardens, Field and Nile,* and *Red Sea Digest.*"

6 Boaz—"He'll never be ruthless."

5 Ezra—"He's got the write stuff, baby."

4 King Xerxes—"The candidate with Esther-vescence."

3 Nebuchadnezzer—"Vote for me . . . or else."

2 Pontius Pilate—"When it comes to crime, he's not wishy-washy."

1 Caesar—"Don't leave Rome without him."

Who is the greatest baby-sitter mentioned in the Bible?

Answer

David. He rocked Goliath to sleep.

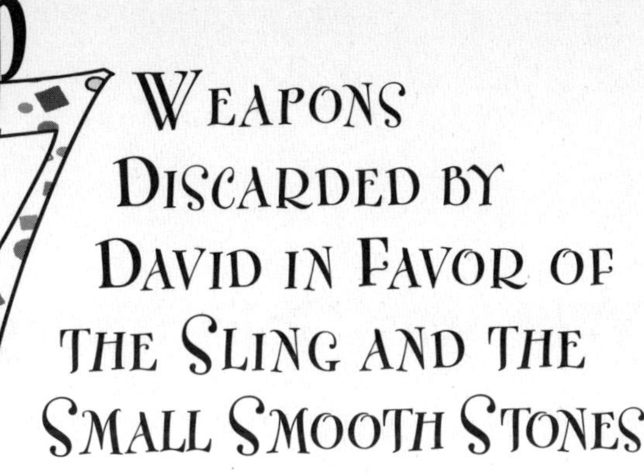

Top 7 Weapons Discarded by David in Favor of the Sling and the Small Smooth Stones

7 Flaming harp ("Lyre, lyre, ball of fire")

6 Banana peel

5 The "Look out behind you!" trick

4 Bad cheese sandwich and curdled goat's milk

3 Poisonous sheep

2 Fruitcake

1 Giant wedgie

Why was Goliath surprised when David hurled the small smooth stone at him?

Answer

Because such a thing had never entered his head before.

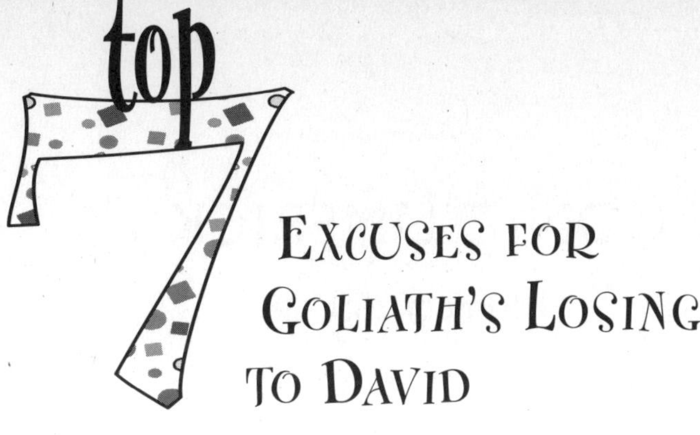

Excuses for Goliath's Losing to David

7 He was feeling flustered after being called an "uncircumcised Philistine."

6 He lost the stone in the sun.

5 When he heard that David had picked up five stones, he misunderstood and thought David was bringing "scones."

4 He was distracted by a high-pitched whistle only he could hear (1 Samuel 17:41–43).

3 He felt woozy after eating bad mutton for lunch.

2 He fell for the old "Your sandal is untied" routine.

1 The battle instructions for defending against slingshots were in Japanese.

LACONIC LIMERICK #5

I Samuel 25:1–38

Nabal is known as a fool,
To all he was wicked and cruel,
But one fatal mistake
he couldn't unmake,
refusing the one who would rule.

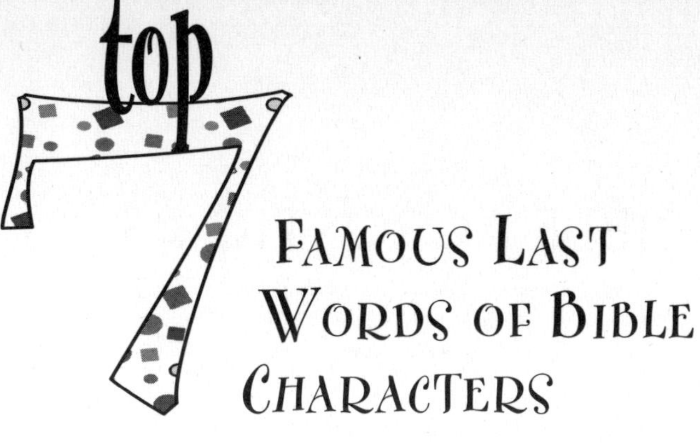

Famous Last Words of Bible Characters

7 The people of Jericho before the walls came a tumblin' down: "My mother plays better trumpet than that."

6 Balaam's talking donkey: "I dedicate my body to science and my jawbone to Samson."

5 Goliath: "Ouch!"

4 Solomon, to his seven hundredth wife: "You're the only woman I've ever really loved."

3 Thomas, after being informed that he was dying: "I doubt it!"

2 John the Baptist: "This queen is a pain in the neck!"

1 Ananias and Sapphira after holding back money from God: "The Lord helps those who help themselves."

BIBLE ACROSTIC #5

David's mighty men could have called themselves HARPS:

Hard-core

Army to

Really

Pound

Saul

top 7 Biblical Pets

7 Adam and Eve—that cute little furry beast that Adam hasn't named yet

6 Noah—pair of partridges in a bare tree

5 Joseph—peacock (bird of many colors)

4 Job—baby behemoth (Job 40:15)

3 Jonah—very small fish

2 Saul in Damascus—seeing-eye dog

1 Jesus—lost and found sheep

SALESMEN, BASEBALL PLAYERS, OR FARMERS?

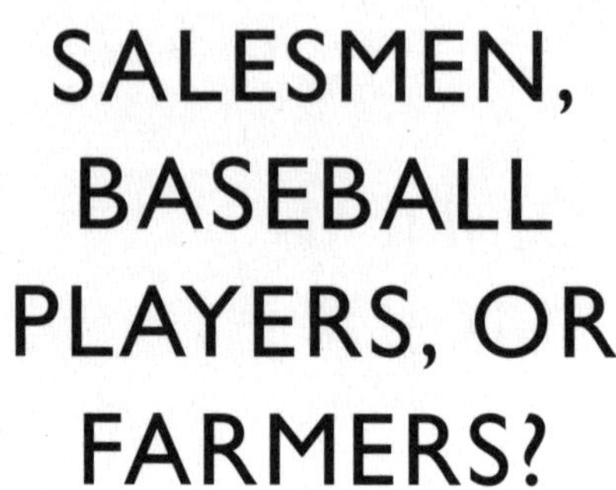

"So Israel and Absalom pitched in the land of Gilead."

(2 Samuel 17:26, KJV)

Top 7 Elements of Conventional Wisdom

7 If God wanted me to touch my toes, he would have put them on my knees.

6 Remember: Amateurs built the ark. Experts built the *Titanic*.

5 The Golden Rule is useless unless you realize that it is your move.

4 There is always a lot to be thankful for if you take the time to look for it. For example, I'm sitting here thinking how nice it is that wrinkles don't hurt.

3 We have thirty-five million laws to enforce the Ten Commandments.

2 Thousands of years ago, cats were worshiped as gods. Cats have never forgotten this.

1 A man who says marriage is a fifty-fifty proposition doesn't understand two things: (1) women, and (2) fractions.

Where is the first sports car mentioned in Scripture?

Answer

Throughout the land was heard the noise of David's triumph.

Top 7 Titles Rejected by David in Favor of "Mighty Men"

7 Dave and His Posse (too modern)

6 The Warm Fuzzies (too cute)

5 The Whole Hee-Haw Gang (too overused)

4 The Mod Squad (it had potential)

3 A Bunch of Really Great Guys Who Killed a Lot of People (pretty accurate but a little long)

2 The Imperials (everyone else has been a part of that music group, why not them?)

1 Dream Team (good, but Mighty Men was just a little better)

Where did they first sleep five in a bed?

Answer

David slept with his forefathers.

(1 Kings 2:10)

Top 7 Pet Peeves of King Solomon

7 Having people ask, "If you're so smart, why haven't you been on *Jeopardy?*"

6 Being asked the names of all his wives and children

5 Finding Christmas cards large enough for the names of everyone in his family

4 Signing Christmas cards

3 Being a tourist attraction (1 Kings 4:34)

2 Not being able to find the tune to "Song of Solomon"

1 Having all those mothers-in-law

NEW METHODS OF EVANGELISM—I

PYRAMID EVANGELISM (AKA MULTILEVEL EVANGELISM)—Organize ten people to reach ten other people to share Christ with others, who organize ten other people, and so on. You don't have to actually talk with any pagans yourself, but you'll get all the credit since the process originated with you.

Top 7 New Year's Resolutions of King Solomon

7 To only propose twenty-seven times this year

6 To spend more time with his children—or at least get their names straight

5 To take better care of his cuticles

4 To double his fish intake—it's brain food, you know

3 To put scented soap, candles, and potpourri in all palace bathrooms

2 To write another song (see Song of Solomon)

1 To get a new vanity (see Ecclesiastes)

LACONIC LIMERICK #6

2 Kings 2:23–24

There once was a man with no hairs
who endured youthful mocking and stares,
But he was not deterred
and then had the last word,
as the boys became sport for the bears.

Words Not Found in Scripture

7 Groovy, as in, "Wow, man, that vision was groovy!"

6 Scrumpdilyitious, as in, "My, this manna is scrumpdilyitious!"

5 Input, as in, "Hey, Moses, I need your input on this."

4 Yowser, as in David's response when he saw Bathsheba, "Yowser!"

3 Internet, as in Peter's instructions, "Hey, John, toss that Internet on the other side of the boat."

2 Schwepervescence, as in, "Therefore, rid yourselves of all malice and all deceit, hypocrisy, envy, and schwepervescence." (1 Peter 2:1)

1 Threepeat, as in, "will the Damascus Roadwings threepeat?"

BIBLE ACROSTIC #6

Elisha's "group of prophets"
(see 2 Kings 4:38, NLT)
could have been called SEERS:

Special
Envoys
Explaining
Righteous
Stuff

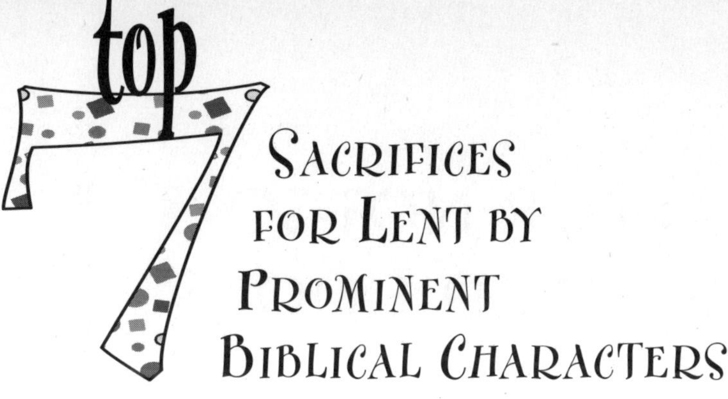

Sacrifices for Lent by Prominent Biblical Characters

7 Adam—fresh fruit

6 Esau—Campbell's Hearty Pottage

5 Nabal—strong drink (1 Samuel 25:36–38)

4 David—daily rooftop visits

3 Absalom—low branches

2 Haman—banquets

1 Ezekiel—"wheat, barley, beans, lentils, millet, and spelt" (Ezekiel 4:9, NLT)

FOR NOT-SO-GOOD COOKS

"O thou man of God,
there is death in
the pot!"

(2 Kings 4:40, KJV)

Sports in Bible Olympics

7 Lamb hurling

6 Garment rending

5 500-meter hyssop purge (Hebrews 9:19)

4 5,000-meter Dead Sea float

3 Prophet chase (1 Kings 19:1–4)

2 Downhill shalom

1 Ship race from Fair Havens to Malta (Acts 27:8–28:1)

LACONIC LIMERICK #7

2 Kings 5:1–19

Naaman, a desperate man,
said to Elisha, "Please do what you can,"
When seven times he went in,
so clear was his skin,
that he quickly became a God-fan.

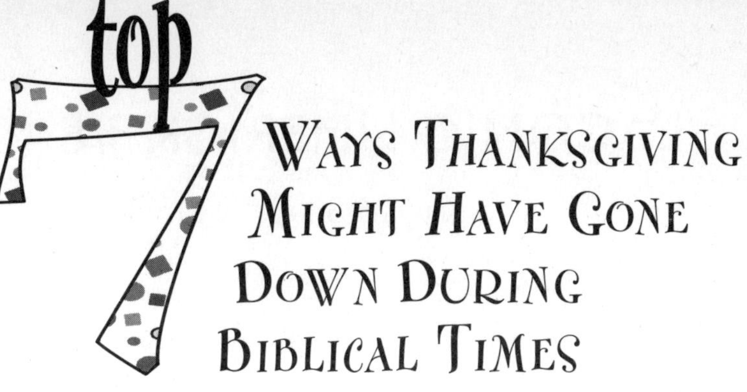

Top 7 Ways Thanksgiving Might Have Gone Down During Biblical Times

7 Chariot jams on the way to Grandma's house

6 Young Israelite boys with slingshots shooting at the giant inflatable Caesar balloons that highlight every Phatama's Thanksgiving day parade (Phatama, a holiday tradition for sixty years)

5 Roasted camel leftovers. (Would you like the hump or a leg?)

4 No meal would be complete without an appetizer tray consisting of kumquat dip, those little round sausages that everybody likes but nobody knows what they're called, and Kentucky-fried dove.

3 Ahkmed-seltzer, helping heartburn sufferers for three score and seven years

2 Men bonding after dinner while watching rip-roaring gladiator games on television

1 Women suddenly having the urge to go to the Jerusalem manufacturers' marketplace the next day

LACONIC LIMERICK #8

2 Kings 9:34–37

Jezebel the queen was a hog,
She lived in a morality fog,
But when stripped of her power
and thrown from the tower,
she made a nice meal for a dog.

Where is tennis mentioned in the Bible?

Answer

"And it came to pass, afore Isaiah was gone out into the middle court." (2 Kings 20:4, KJV)

top 7 Biblical Recipes

7 Eve's Forbidden-Fruit Salad: a real eyeopener

6 Moses' Manna Cotti: given to Italy by the Catholic Church in 1592

5 Elijah's Blackened Beef: enough to impress even the most pagan guests

4 John the Baptist's Honey Bunches o' Bugs: great on those long wilderness journeys!

3 Judas's Devil's Food Cake: looks tempting, but watch the aftereffects (eternal heartburn)

2 Peter's Gentile Casserole: a blend of unclean meats cooked in a sheet

1 Jesus' Bread of Life: eat with a glass of living water and never hunger or thirst again!

"YOU WASH . . . I'LL DRY"

"I will wipe Jerusalem
as a man wipeth
a dish, wiping it,
and turning it
upside down."

(2 Kings 21:13, KJV)

Top 7 Enemies of Israel Not Mentioned in Scripture

7 Moabetterites

6 Startafites

5 What-a-bites

4 Parasites

3 Cellulites

2 Fraidaheights

1 Menintites

THOUGHT FOR THE DAY

"At Parbar westward,
four at the causeway,
and two at Parbar."

(1 Chronicles 26:18, KJV)

Top 7 Merchants of the Jericho Road Mall

7 Body by Samson and Hair by Delilah

6 Goliath's Big and Tall Shop

5 Esther's Queen-Sized Apparel

4 Ezekiel's Wheels 'R' Us

3 John B's Health Foods—specializing in locusts and honey

2 Zaccheus R. Block Tax Preparation

1 Judas's Coin Collectors Hangout (now having a 30 percent off sale)

GOD'S PEOPLE NEED TO BE ON TIME!

"But let none come into the house of the LORD, save the priests, and they that minister of the Levites; they shall go in, for they are holy: but all the people shall keep the watch of the LORD."

(2 Chronicles 23:6, KJV)

IS IT TRUE THAT THE HITTITES WERE CARPENTERS? (HIT TIGHTS)—SEE JUDGES 3:5

the Gittites were ballerinas?
(get tights)—see 2 Samuel 15:18
and the Shuhites were cobblers?
(shoe-hites)—Job 8:1

top 7 Completely Untrue Biblical Tabloid Stories

7 Archaeological dig at Bethlehem manger proves the little drummer boy was actually the Energizer bunny.

6 Balaam's donkey sang "Don't Be Cruel" with Elvis's voice.

5 Noah's ark discovered in a New Jersey warehouse.

4 Fossilized whale skeleton found with the words "Jonah was here" etched on a rib.

3 All three "wise" men failed Astronomy 101.

2 Nebuchadnezzar gave milk (see Daniel 4:33).

1 Cannibals fed up with missionaries.

SHORTEST MAN IN THE BIBLE, PART ONE

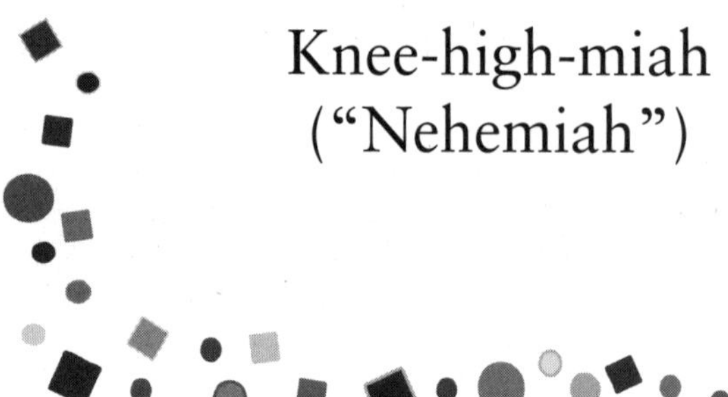

Knee-high-miah
("Nehemiah")

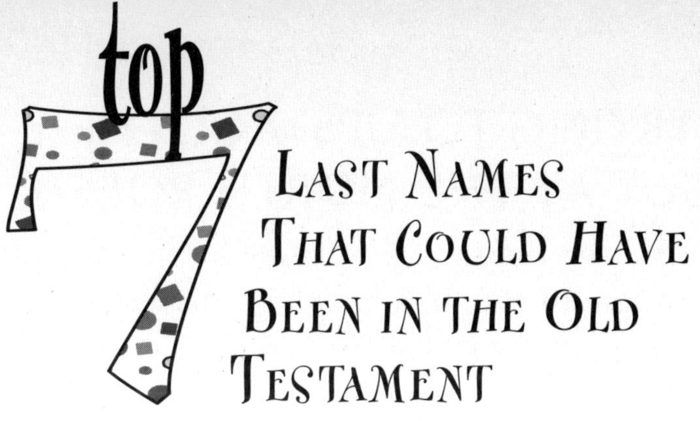

Top 7 Last Names That Could Have Been in the Old Testament

7 Abel *Bodied*

6 Noah *More*

5 Esau *You*

4 Miriam *Off*

3 Jethro *Theball*

2 Achan *Back*

1 Jezebel *Ringer*

TRYING TO UPSTAGE THE GUY AT THE NORTH POLE?

"And the king . . . proclaimed a holiday throughout the provinces and distributed gifts with royal liberality."

(Esther 2:18)

LACONIC LIMERICK #9

Job 1

Of all in the world, he was best,
with wealth and family blessed.
Then hit with Satan's afflictions
and friends' derelictions,
Whatever, Job passed the test!

TALK ABOUT A PRECOCIOUS BABY!

Job cursed the day he was born. (Job 3:3)

top 7 Sandwiches Served at the Jerusalem Grill

7 The Adam—a half-slab of ribs, marinated with apple juice, and served open-face on your choice of three tempting homemade breads

6 Noah's Ultimate Combo Plate—your choice of two helpings of everything on the menu

5 The David—a hero sandwich

4 Goliath's Real Manwich Belly Buster

3 The Lazarus—a three-day-old "po'" boy special

2 The Peter Burger—there's no denying the taste

1 The Judas Iscariot—costs thirty pieces of silver, but the flavor hangs around

FIVE O'CLOCK SHADOW?

"Wilt thou pursue the dry stubble?"

(Job 13:25, KJV)

SHORTEST MAN IN THE BIBLE, PART TWO

Bildad the Shuhite ("shoe height")

(Job 8:1)

Books of the Bible That Never Were

7 The Book of Job—for those seeking a career change

6 The Book of Noah—too boring (hammer a peg, pour some pitch, hammer a peg, pour some pitch . . .)

5 The Book of Collisions—where the sin is repaired to make it look like it never happened

4 The Book of Hesitations—for those undecided souls

3 The Book of Paul—the letter to himself

2 Fourth John—the next generation

1 The unfinished Gospel According to Judas

How do we know that Job went to a chiropractor?

Answer

"I was at ease, but he hath broken me asunder: he hath also taken me by my neck, and shaken me to pieces, and set me up for his mark." (Job 16:12, KJV)

Slogans for Biblical Schools of Higher Learning

7 Abraham College—"We don't make graduates; we make nations."

6 The Davidic School of Music—"Music fit for a king."

5 Solomon University—"The best place to get your M.R.S. degree."

4 Philistine Institute of Technology—"We stand head and shoulders above the rest."

3 Delilah's School of Beauty—"We bring men to their knees."

2 Satan's Party College—"Our programs are a blast, but graduating is hell."

1 Heaven University—"Our degrees are eternal, and plenty of scholarships are available."

"USED RIGHT GUARD, BUT FORGOT TO USE LEFT GUARD"

"Canst thou make
him afraid as a
grasshopper? The
glory of his nostrils
is terrible."

(Job 39:20, KJV)

Top 7 Mythical Bible Web Sites

7 www.bulznlambs.org (Levites)

6 www.fleece.com (Gideon)

5 www.SAM-I-AM.org (Samuel)

4 www.bookman.edu (Ezra)

3 www.fishers.net (Peter)

2 www.apostletoo.com (Paul)

1 www.kingme.gov (Herod)

TOO MUCH JUNK MAIL ISN'T NEW

"Who can come within
his double mail?"

(Job 41:13, NASB)

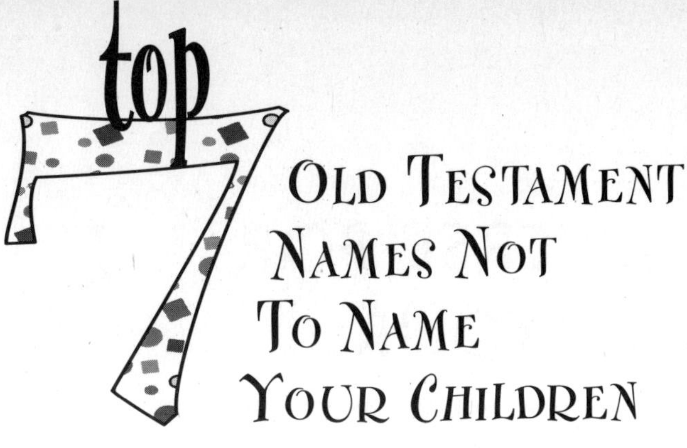

Top 7 Old Testament Names Not to Name Your Children

7 Achan (Joshua 7)

6 Ichabod (1 Samuel 4:21)

5 Jezebel (1 Kings 16–22)

4 Manasseh (2 Kings 21)

3 Pashhur (Jeremiah 20)

2 Oholah (Ezekiel 23)

1 Gomer (Hosea 1)

A VERSE FOR YOUR DENTIST

"Open wide your mouth and I will fill it."

(Psalm 81:10)

top 7 Quotes from Biblical Moms

7 Joseph's Mom—"Joey, you're such a dreamer!"

6 Moses' Mom—"Look both ways before crossing the Red Sea."

5 Samson's Mom—"What's it gonna take—an eye?"

4 Goliath's Mom—"You may be nine feet tall, young man, but I can still put you over my knee!"

3 Solomon's Mom—"Oh, you think you're so smart!"

2 Pontius Pilate's Mom—"Look at those hands. They're filthy!"

1 Paul's Mom—"Why is it you can write letters to everyone else but never to your mother?"

SOMETHING NOT TO SAY WHILE YOUR WIFE IS HAVING BAD LABOR PAINS

The Bible says, "A woman giving birth to a child has pain because her time has come; but when her baby is born she forgets the anguish.

(John 16:21)

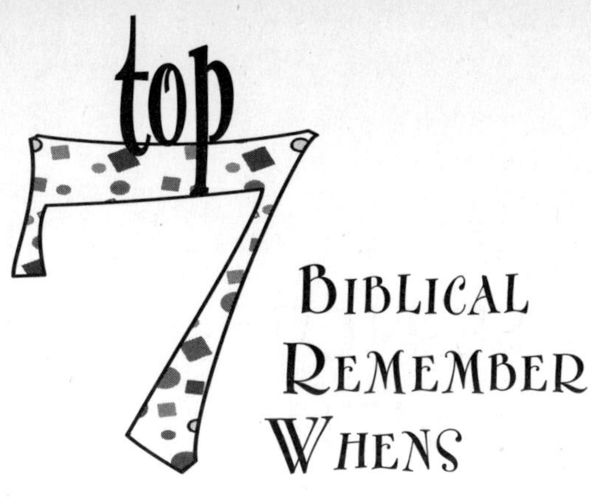

Top 7 Biblical Remember Whens

7 Adam—"I remember the lonely singles scene."

6 Eve—"I remember when finding an outfit to wear took no time at all."

5 King Solomon—"I remember when married life was simple."

4 Jezebel—"I remember in high school when I was voted Miss Congeniality."

3 Zacchaeus—"I remember coining the phrase 'shortchanged.'"

2 Peter—"I remember the unique taste of foot (as 'in my mouth')."

1 Judas—"I remember when everyone trusted me."

A VERSE NOT TO USE WITH A WEDDING GIFT

"A nagging wife is as annoying as the constant dripping on a rainy day."

(Proverbs 27:15, NLT)

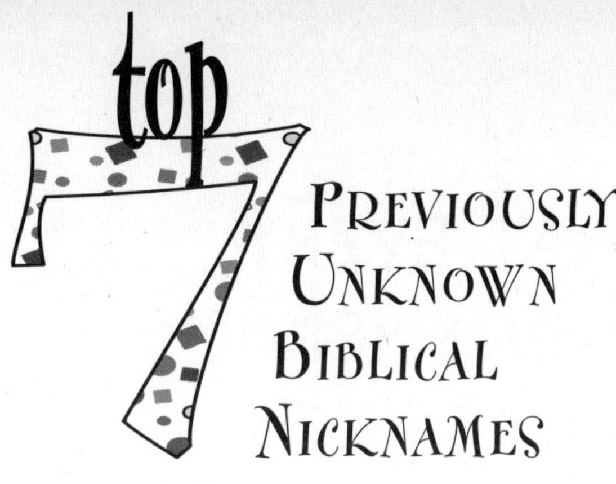

Top 7 Previously Unknown Biblical Nicknames

7 Noah and sons Shem, Ham, and Japeth were known as the Skipper, Mr. Howell, Professor, and Gilligan.

6 Moses was often called the Moes Man, The Moester, Mr. Manna, Mannameister, and Mos-erama.

5 Elijah and Elisha were known as Big E and Little E.

4 Few people know that Shadrach, Meshach, and Abednego were affectionately referred to by their friends as Rare, Medium, and Well Done.

3 Behind his back, Isaiah was known as Hot Lips.

2 Everyone has heard of Doubting Thomas, but what about "Not Entirely Clear on the Subject" Matthias?

1 John Mark was called "the Streak" (see Mark 14:51–52).

WHAT EVERY PUBLISHER WANTS TO HEAR

"Of making many books there is no end."

(Ecclesiastes 12:12)

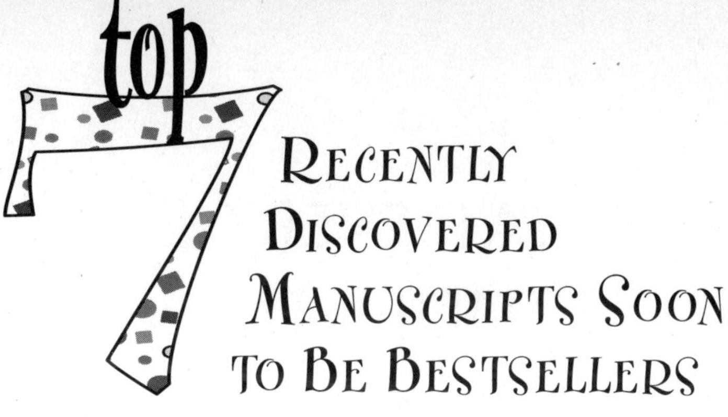

Top 7 Recently Discovered Manuscripts Soon to Be Bestsellers

7 *The Joys of Self-Control*—Cain

6 *Games to Play on Long Trips*—Noah

5 *Fish Bait: What to Use and What to Avoid (Namely, Yourself)*—Jonah

4 *The Ultimate Health Food Cookbook*—John the Baptist (featuring items readily available in the backyard)

3 *The Art of Fencing*—Peter

2 *Very Hot Investing Tips*—Ananias and Sapphira

1 *Traveling Light on a Tight Budget*—Paul

WHAT EVERY STUDENT KNOWS

"Much study wearies the body."

(Ecclesiastes 12:12)

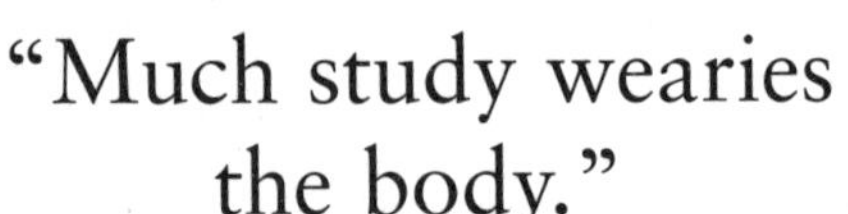

Top 7 Bible Bumper Stickers

7 My Other Vehicle Is a Chariot.

6 Have You Hugged Your Pharisee Today?

5 I'd Rather Be Fishing for Men!

4 I Brake for Blinding Lights on the Road to Damascus.

3 If You Can Read This, You're Standing in Donkey Doo.

2 Just Say No to Tax Collectors.

1 Don't Laugh, at Least This Donkey's Paid For.

A VERSE NOT TO USE IN A GET-WELL CARD

"From the sole of the foot
even unto the head there is
no soundness in it; but
wounds, and bruises, and
putrifying sores: they have
not been closed, neither
bound up, neither mollified
with ointment."

(Isaiah 1:6, KJV)

Biblical Candies

7 The choice of the Trinity—The Three Musketeers

6 Created on the third day, there's Milky Way

5 For those undecided souls—Twix

4 The Sadducees' favorite—Snickers

3 For the spiritually immature—Sugar Babies

2 The candy bar of the tribulation—Pay Day

1 The choice of the redeemed—Life Saver

A VERSE NOT TO PLACE OVER THE ENTRANCE TO A RESTAURANT

"For all tables are full of vomit and filthiness, so that there is no place clean."

(Isaiah 28:8, KJV)

Top 7 Ancient Talk Show Subjects (If They Had Talk Shows)

7 Did Adam have a belly button?

6 What's with all this talk about Babel?

5 Prophetic donkeys—the government's next $12 million study

4 Was Goliath a mama's boy?

3 Women who act like Jezebel and the men who fear them

2 Haman's hang-ups

1 Getting down with Jeremiah

A VERSE NOT TO USE AS A CHURCH MOTTO

"Listen, you foolish
and senseless people—
who have eyes but do
not see, who have
ears but do not hear."

(Jeremiah 5:21, NLT)

top 7 Things Not to Try at Home!

7 "A woman dropped an upper millstone on his head and cracked his skull." (Judges 9:53)

6 "So he went out and caught three hundred foxes and tied them tail to tail in pairs. He then fastened a torch to every pair of tails." (Judges 15:4)

5 "He picked up a burning coal with a pair of tongs. He touched my lips with it." (Isaiah 6:6–7, NLT)

4 "Take the girdle that thou hast got, which is upon thy loins, and arise, go to Euphrates, and hide it there in a hole of the rock." (Jeremiah 13:4, KJV)

3 "So I opened my mouth, and he gave me the scroll to eat. Then he said to me, 'Son of man, eat this scroll I am giving you and fill your stomach with it.'" (Ezekiel 3:2–3)

2 "Son of man, take a sharp sword and use it as a razor to shave your head and beard." (Ezekiel 5:1, NLT)

1 "Then from his mouth the serpent spewed water like a river, to overtake the woman and sweep her away with the torrent." (Revelation 12:15)

Who was the first drug addict in the Bible?

Answer

Nebuchadnezzar—he was on grass for seven years. (Daniel 4:31–33)

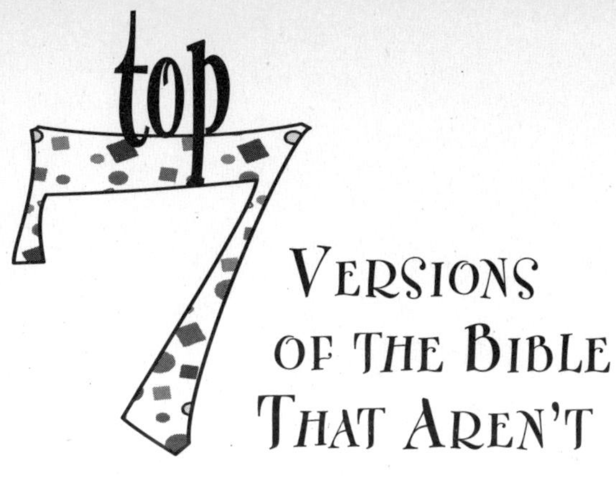

Versions of the Bible That Aren't

7 Re-revised Old Version King James, Living International, Nonsexist, Amplified, American Standard yet accepted by the U.N. Bible

6 The Schwartzenegger edition, where Jesus said, "I'll be back"

5 Modern Name Edition, where those hard-to-pronounce biblical names have been replaced with names like Vince, Biff, and Nigel

4 The Spielberg Bible

3 Multiple-Choice Version, where each scripture command now has three or four additional options from which you can make a choice that best suits your lifestyle

2 Scratch-and-Sniff Edition

1 Pencil-Print Edition—If you don't like what it says, just grab your eraser.

LACONIC LIMERICK #10

Hosea 1–3

When Hosea took Gomer as wife,
he knew there'd be trouble and strife.
And then when she strayed,
faithful he stayed,
modeling God's grace with his life.

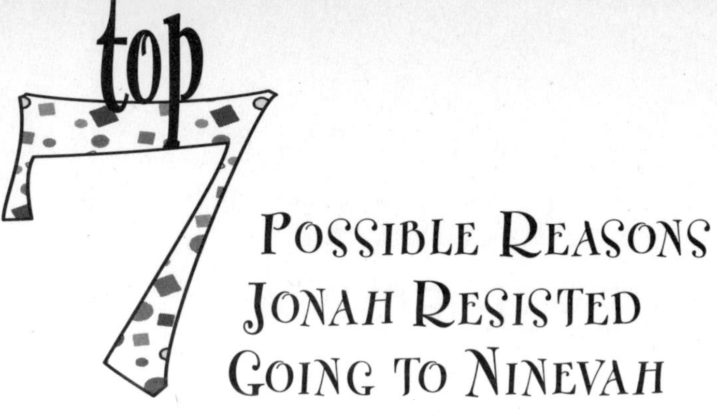

Top 7 Possible Reasons Jonah Resisted Going to Ninevah

7 He was unhappy with his passport photo.

6 He'd get more frequent sailing miles if he went to Tarshish instead.

5 He would lose his deposit on his upcoming weekend fishing trip.

4 They had free HBO at the Tarshish Motel 6.

3 He wanted to renegotiate his per diem travel allowance.

2 At a crossroads, some joker switched the Ninevah and Tarshish directional signs.

1 He had allergies to sackcloth and ashes and a severe aversion to torture and death.

A GREAT VERSE FOR AN OPTOMETRIST

"I will . . . make you a spectacle."

(Nahum 3:6)

top 7 Bible Characters and Their Cars

7 Adam and Eve—a Viper

6 Jacob—a Grand Caravan (the extended length provides plenty of room for two wives, two handmaids, and twelve boys)

5 Moses—a Hummer (great for those wilderness journeys)

4 Balaam—a Lincoln Mark VIII (with voice warning—he loves transportation that talks)

3 Elijah—a Corvette ZR1 (let's see Jezebel and her chariot catch this one)

2 John the Baptist—the new Volkswagen Beetle (what else for a guy who eats bugs?)

1 The Twelve Apostles—a Honda (remember, they were all in one accord—Acts 2:1, KJV)

THE WORST GET-WELL CARD EVER

"Nothing can heal
your wound;
your injury is fatal.
Everyone who hears
the news about you
claps his hands at
your fall."

(Nahum 3:19)

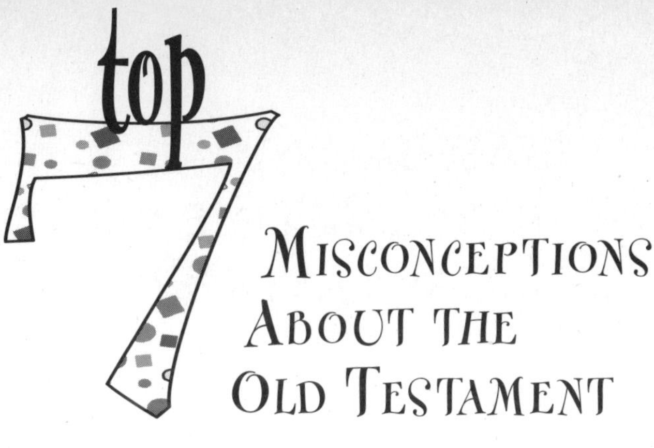

Top 7 Misconceptions About the Old Testament

7 The judges of Israel included Wopner and Judge Judy.

6 Delilah gave Samson the first Mohawk.

5 Speaking of Samson, his descendants were called Samsonites, destined to become luggage makers.

4 Starbucks Middle East carried Manna in three exciting flavors—chocolate latté, banana mocha, and tangy passion fruit.

3 David wrote a psalm called “Ode to the Flugelhorn.”

2 Jacob’s son, Levi, was the father of blue jeans.

1 Eve wasn’t blond.

BASEBALL . . . AMERICAN PASTIME OR BIBLICAL PASTIME?

In the beginning ("big inning") . . .

—Genesis 1:1

Eve took first.

—Genesis 3:6

Adam stole second.

—Genesis 3:6

Gideon rattled the pitchers.

—Judges 7:16

The prodigal son made a home run.

—Luke 15:20

April Fool's Day Pranks Not Recorded in Scripture

7 To alleviate stress on the ark, Shem, Ham, and Japheth put the two skunks under Noah's cot.

6 Moses parted the Red Sea just as Aaron jumped off the diving board.

5 Moses threw his rod down during one of Miriam's Bible studies, and she didn't like snakes.

4 In the cave, David not only cut off part of Saul's robe, but he also tied his sandal laces together!

3 Paul pretended to have "writer's block."

2 Solomon's secretary gave him the ambiguous message, "Your wife called."

1 When King Agrippa wouldn't convert, Paul put a whoopee cushion on his throne.

The New Testament

In New Testament times, why would shepherds refuse to hang-glide?

Answer

They were sore ["soar"] afraid.

(Luke 2:9, KJV)

Reasons the Inn Was Full on Christmas Eve

7 It was offering a Weekend Special—Kids and animals sleep for free.

6 It had experienced a surge in popularity since receiving a AAA four-diamond rating.

5 Joseph couldn't decide if 10-10-321 or 1-800-COLLECT was the best way to phone in the reservation.

4 It was the last exit before the next oasis.

3 The light was off at the nearest Motel 6.

2 Herod was sponsoring a weekend conference on child rearing.

1 The Y0K bug had messed up most inn reservation systems.

FLIGHT TO EGYPT

After Sunday school, a little boy proudly displayed to his parents the picture he had drawn in class. It looked very much like an airplane with passengers, so his father asked what the picture represented.

"It's the 'flight to Egypt,'" answered the boy.

"I see," said his father, "and this must be Mary and the baby Jesus."

"Yes!" the son answered enthusiastically.

"Who's flying the plane?" Dad asked, pointing to the cockpit.

Without skipping a beat, the boy answered, "That's Pontius, the pilot!"

"I see," said Dad. Then pointing to a rotund figure in the back of the plane, he asked, "Who's this?"

"That's Round John Virgin!"

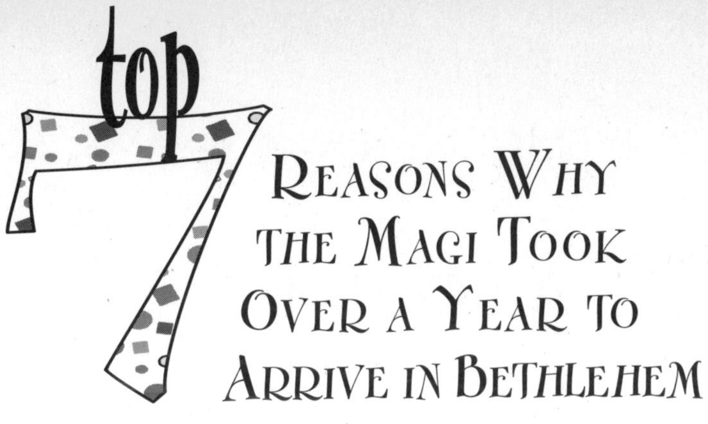

Top 7 Reasons Why the Magi Took Over a Year to Arrive in Bethlehem

7 Got stuck in the drive-thru at Burger Pharaoh

6 Wanted to be fashionably late

5 Spent time waiting for Curly, the fourth wise guy, who never showed up

4 Were busy at the Magi convention

3 Didn't want to be caught in the Christmas rush

2 Wanted to wait for Jesus to be out of the manger due to Gaspar's hay fever

1 Couldn't decide whether to bring gold, frankincense, and myrrh or the clapper, a breadmaker, and a Thighmaster

A SOCIAL FAUX PAS

"And when the Pharisee saw it, he marvelled that he had not first washed before dinner."

(Luke 11:38, KJV)

top 7 Things Overheard at the Sermon on the Mount

7 "Down in front!"

6 "Martha, why didn't we bring the lawn chairs?"

5 "Quit hogging the program!"

4 "What seminary did this guy go to anyway?"

3 "Are they gonna hit us up for an offering at the end of this thing?"

2 "What did he say? Blessed are the cheese makers?"

1 "Peanuts, popcorn, unleavened bread . . ."

Why did people stop asking Zacchaeus for a loan?

Answer

Because he was always a little short.

(Luke 19:1–4)

Ways to Peg a False Messiah

7 Charges 15 percent gratuity for multitudes of ten or more

6 Bread of life tastes remarkably similar to a Slimfast bar

5 Is currently being investigated by the IRS

4 Has a 1-900 number

3 Distributes genuine Holy Land cookbooks that are made in Taiwan

2 Says, "Sell all that you have and give it to me."

1 Refuses to preach on Luke 21

LACONIC LIMERICK #11

Luke 19:1–10

Climbing the tree, some thought strange,
Some even mentioned derange,
He must have heard their retort,
"You're just a bit short!"
but then Christ gave Zacchaeus some change.

BIBLE ACROSTIC #8

The Pharisees could have used the name LAWS:

Let's
All
Whack
Someone

New Testament Vanity Plates

7 4 RUN R—John the Baptist

6 GYL ES—Nathanael (John 1:47, KJV)

5 I C U 2—former blind man healed by Jesus (Mark 8:22–24)

4 D CON—Stephen

3 BUDDY—Barnabas

2 N10 SE—Priscilla

1 NSPYRD—John on the island of Patmos

LACONIC LIMERICK #12

John 6:3–13

Their once was a boy with a lunch
who thought to himself, "I've a hunch,
if I give to this Man
all that I can
with my little, he'll make a bunch!"

A VERSE NOT TO USE IN MARRIAGE COUNSELING

"This woman is driving me crazy."

(Luke 18:5, NLT)

Rejected Original Disciples

7 Raul the Goat Herder

6 José the Caesarean Jailer

5 Marcus the Gravedigger

4 Scully the Gourmet Ship Cook

3 Pablo the Most Excellent Tailor

2 Fred the Fearless Gladiator

1 Big Vinnie the Grape Stomper

BIBLE ACROSTIC #9

An organization of lepers could have been entitled PARTS:

People

Admitting

Really

Terrible

Sores

A VERSE NOT TO HAVE ON YOUR TOMBSTONE

"And it came to pass, that the beggar died."

(Luke 16:22, KJV)

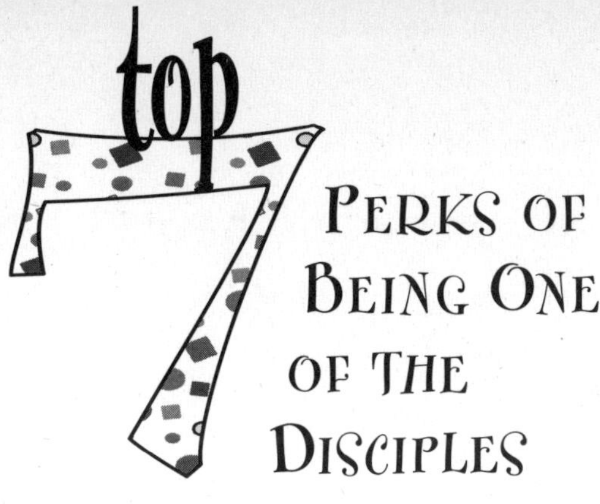

Top 7 Perks of Being One of the Disciples

7 Knowing the secret disciple handshake

6 Backstage pass to Jesus' sermons

5 Free sandals and foot washings as needed

4 Free parable interpretations (no commentaries back then)

3 Having a tax collector on their side for a change

2 Get to mock the Pharisees

1 All the loaves and fish they can eat

BIBLE ACROSTIC #10

Jesus' disciples could have called themselves HITS:

Having an

Inside

Track to the

Savior

or the GUYS:

Gaining

Understanding

You

See

TRAVEL ADVICE

"But pray ye that your flight be not in the winter, neither on the sabbath day."

(Matthew 24:20, KJV)

Parables That Weren't

7 The Parable of the Wise Sheep

6 The Parable of the Ketchup Seed

5 The Parable of the Bad Samaritan

4 The Parable of the Lost Wool Sweater

3 The Parable of the Fig Tree that Bore Fig Newtons

2 The Parable of the Man Who Built His House on a Sand Trap (for frustrated golfers)

1 The Parable of the Rich Man Who Got Stuck Going through the Eye of a Needle

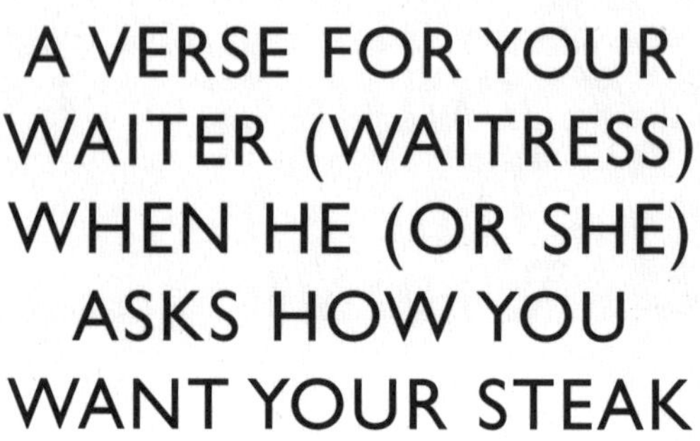

A VERSE FOR YOUR WAITER (WAITRESS) WHEN HE (OR SHE) ASKS HOW YOU WANT YOUR STEAK

"Well done, good and faithful servant!"

(Matthew 25:21)

New Year's Resolutions of Judas

7 To lose thirty pounds

6 To stop saying "And, um" and "Swell"

5 Not to take any marked coins

4 To be nicer to people

3 To pay up his life insurance

2 To stop investing in failed S&L's

1 Not to kiss and tell

THEME VERSE FOR THE IRS

"Whoever does not
have, even what he
has will be taken
from him."

(Matthew 25:29)

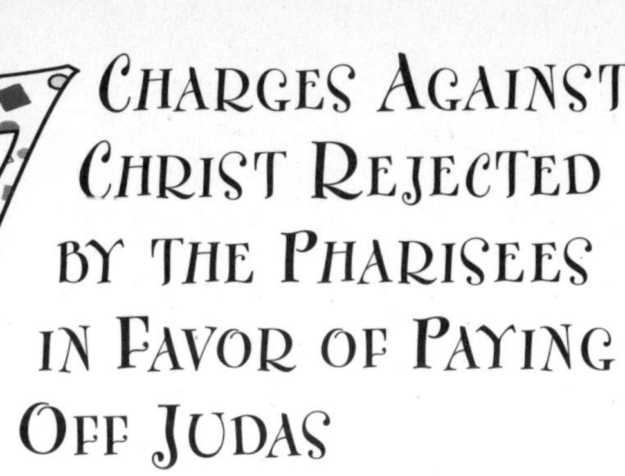

Top 7 Charges Against Christ Rejected by the Pharisees in Favor of Paying Off Judas

7 Tearing the "Do not remove label" off his mattress (didn't work because Jesus had no bed to call his own)

6 Jaywalking in front of the temple (didn't work because traffic lights hadn't been invented yet)

5 Performing miracles without consent of healed individuals (didn't work because they couldn't find anyone who preferred to be sick, lame, or dead)

4 Evading income tax (didn't work because Jesus had no income)

3 Violating fire codes with large crowds (didn't work because Jesus addressed the masses out-of-doors)

2 Associating with questionable people (didn't work because after those people met Jesus, they were changed for the better)

1 Driving without a license (didn't work because Jesus walked everywhere—although he did drive the money-changers out of the temple twice)

What is the smallest sin?

Answer

Flee fornication.
(1 Corinthians 6:18, KJV)

Pet Peeves of Pontius Pilate

7 His wife, Hillary, who thinks she's in charge

6 Always being portrayed by skinny actors with little hair and funny lips

5 Being obligated to let Herod win at Pinochle

4 Just because his name is "Pilate" doesn't mean he can fly a plane

3 Kids not buying his action figure

2 Being called "paunchy" behind his back

1 His hands still not coming clean, even after scrubbing and soaking

A PERFECT VERSE FOR A WEDDING CEREMONY

"Father, forgive these people, because they don't know what they are doing."

(Luke 23:34, NLT)

Top 7 Pet Peeves of the Apostle John

7 Always being listed third after Peter and James

6 You thought Revelation was tough to read, you should have tried writing it

5 People who think his last name is "the Baptist" (that's the other John)

4 Being called "John Boy" by the much older apostles

3 People who skip to the end of Revelation and miss the other twenty-one chapters

2 That nobody knows what John 3:17 says

1 The elders at Ephesus selling the movie rights

THIS PROVES THAT PEOPLE WHO ARE AFRAID TO FLY ARE RIGHT

Jesus said, "Lo, I am with you alway."

(Matthew 28:20, KJV)

If you're high, you're on your own.

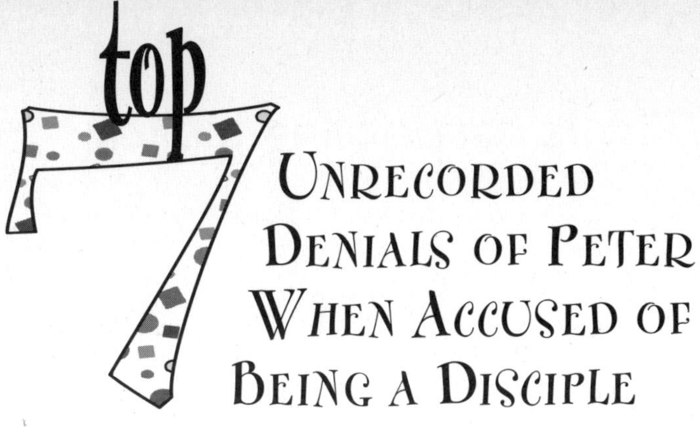

Top 7 Unrecorded Denials of Peter When Accused of Being a Disciple

7 "I wasn't with Jesus. I was just waiting for a bus."

6 "No, now I remember—I was looking for an ATM."

5 "I was just sitting down to get a stone out of my sandal."

4 "I was looking for my contact lens when Jesus happened to walk by."

3 "I was getting in line early for the Fourth of July parade."

2 "I guess I could have been sleepwalking."

1 "You must be confusing me with my identical twin half brother, Payter. I swear it wasn't me!"

Why is carpooling biblical?

Answer

"And when the day of Pentecost was fully come, they were all with one accord in one place." (Acts 2:1, KJV; see also 2 Kings 10:15)

LACONIC LIMERICK #13

Acts 5:1–11

On that strange and eventful day
Ananias and wife came to say,
"Lord, we are giving it all!"
Then down dead they did fall.
What a terrible price to pay!

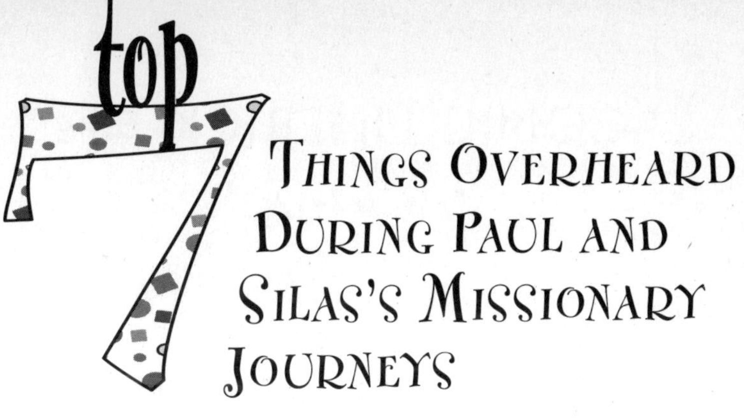

Top 7 Things Overheard During Paul and Silas's Missionary Journeys

7 "What kind of last name is "of Tarsus" anyway?"

6 "Paul, you look a lot taller in person."

5 "Why is it always Paul and Silas? How about Silas and Paul for a change?"

4 "Ohhh, my aching bunions!"

3 "So what does a missionary do for a living?"

2 "Let me get that thorn for you."

1 "What? Stoned again?"

LACONIC LIMERICK #14

Acts 20:7–12

People were packing the place
when Paul spoke, that was often the case,
But not feeling too well,
young Eutychus fell,
And they suddenly met face to face.

A SELF-ESTEEM BOOST FOR THE VERTICALLY CHALLENGED

A short work will the Lord make upon the earth.

(Romans 9:28, KJV)

Top 7 Discomforts of Hell Not Recorded in Scripture

7 Work outfits come in your choice of wool or chain mail.

6 Athlete's foot runs rampant.

5 There's a good supply of canned food but no can openers.

4 All food tastes like cod-liver oil.

3 You're forced to watch continuous *Hee-Haw* reruns.

2 The PA system only plays elevator music.

1 You're continuously asked: "Hot enough for you?"

BIBLICAL PROOF THAT PAUL WAS A SOUTHERNER

Now the God of peace be with you all.

(Romans 15:33, KJV; see also Romans 1:8; 16:24; 1 Corinthians 16:24; 2 Corinthians 2:3, 5; 7:13, 15; 13:14; Ephesians 4:6; 6:21; Philippians 1:4, 7–8; 2:17, 26; 4:23; Colossians 2:13; 4:9; 1 Thessalonians 1:2; 2 Thessalonians 1:3; 3:16, 18; Titus 3:15)

Top 7 Signs of the End-Times Not Recorded in Scripture

7 Spam will be served in fine restaurants everywhere.

6 Professional athletes will agree to play for minimum wage.

5 Everyone will get up one day without hitting their snooze alarm.

4 Things will feel itchier.

3 There will be a dramatic increase in belly-button lint.

2 Global warming will cause all women to have warm feet.

1 The newest NFL franchise will be awarded to Babylon.

THE VEGETARIAN'S CREED

"I will never eat meat again as long as I live."

(1 Corinthians 8:13, NLT)

NEW METHODS OF EVANGELISM—2

CHAIN-LETTER EVANGELISM—Write ten people a letter describing horrible consequences of what will happen to them if they don't get saved and continue the chain.

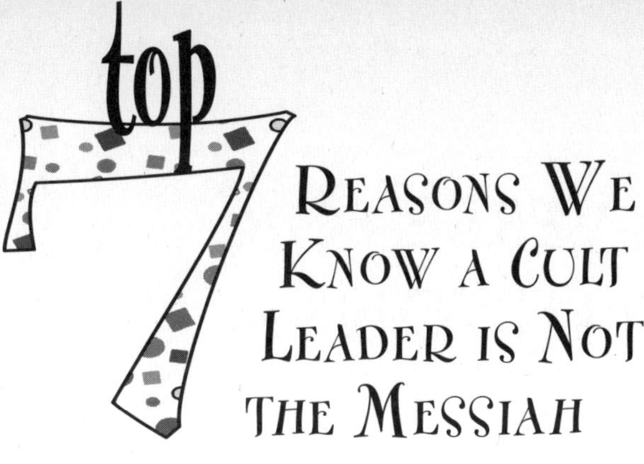

top 7 Reasons We Know a Cult Leader is Not the Messiah

7 He unsuccessfully attempted to resurrect road kill.

6 While trying to walk across the surface of the compound swimming pool, he had to be rescued from the deep end.

5 He was only able to turn water into Kool-Aid.

4 His favorite meal is a ham sandwich.

3 He would rather be fishing for women.

2 He responds to high-pitched sounds that only he can hear.

1 He uses hand puppets in his messages.

A VERSE FOR GLUTTONS—ALL YOU CAN EAT!

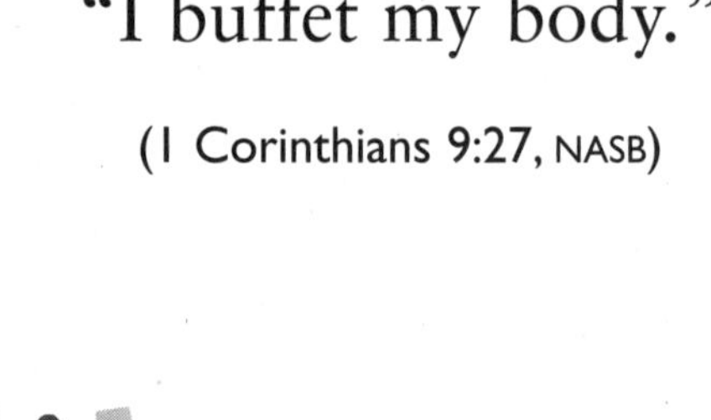

"I buffet my body."

(1 Corinthians 9:27, NASB)

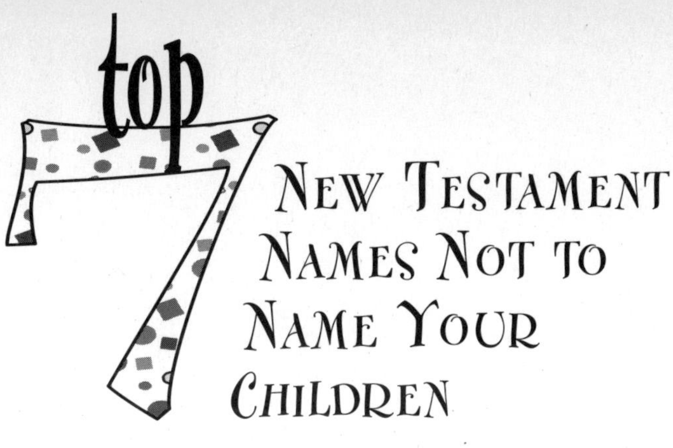

top 7 New Testament Names Not to Name Your Children

7 Judas (Matthew 10)

6 Caiaphas (Matthew 26)

5 Sapphira (Acts 5)

4 Herod (Acts 12)

3 Sceva (Acts 19)

2 Demas (2 Timothy 4:10)

1 Diotrephes (3 John 1)

"What did you learn in church today?" Mom asked her five-year-old.

"We sang a song about a bear with a problem," answered little Suzie.

Intrigued, Mom asked, "Really? What was the name of the song?"

"Gladly, the Cross-eyed Bear," she answered.

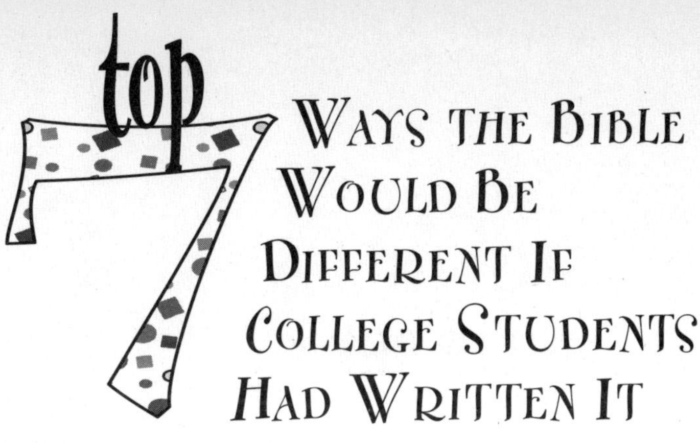

Top 7 Ways the Bible Would Be Different If College Students Had Written It

7 Instead of God creating the world in six days and resting on the seventh, he would have put it off until the night before it was due and then pulled an all-nighter.

6 The reason Cain killed Abel? They were roommates.

5 The Ten Commandments actually number only five, double-spaced, and written in a large font.

4 The reason Moses and the Israelites walked in the desert for forty years? They didn't want to ask for directions and look like freshmen.

3 There's a new edition every two years to limit reselling.

2 Paul's letter to the Romans became Paul's e-mail to the Romans at catacombs@romans.gov.

1 The place where the end of the world occurs is not Armageddon but during finals.

SIGN IN A NURSERY

"We will not all sleep, but we will all be changed."

(1 Corinthians 15:51)

Reasons to Become a Christian

7 Potluck dinners

6 Easy-to-read instruction manual

5 No dues

4 Cheaper than therapy

3 No secret password to learn

2 More brothers and sisters than you can count

1 Great retirement benefits

NEW EVANGELISM METHODS—3

EVANDALISM—Collect rocks, spray paint, knives, and other supplies, then go around town making your faith known. You could spray "Sin stinks!" on bridges and "Jesus saves!" on banks. You could throw rocks through tavern windows with the message "Make a break from sin" attached. You could carve "Be ready for a real homecoming" and an appropriate Bible verse on the football stands. What an impact!

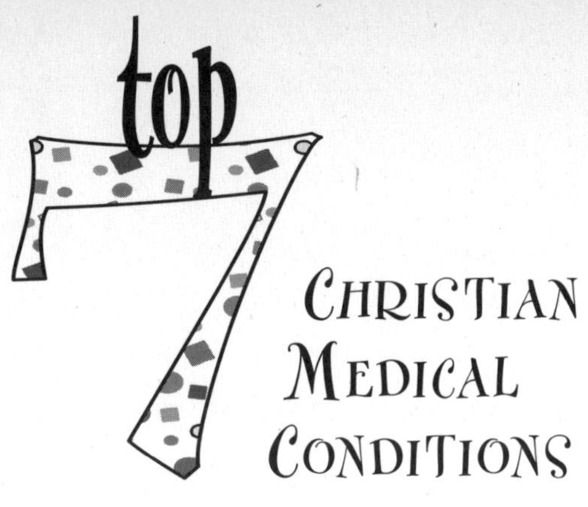

Christian Medical Conditions

7 Those who only pray at meals have "prayergestion."

6 Those who don't read the Word have "constipation of the soul."

5 Those who won't forgive have "hardening of the heart."

4 Those who only attend church twice a year suffer from "biconscience easement."

3 Those who gossip have "hyper-gossipimia."

2 Those who don't tithe have the common condition of "cirrhosis of the giver."

1 Those who fear witnessing suffer from "great commissionaphobia."

One day a little boy said to his mother, "I know what God's name is!"

"Really," replied Mom, "What is it?"

"Art."

"Art?"

"Our Father, Art, in heaven."

Children's Misconceptions About Scripture

7 Jesus lives inside of you and likes pizza, not vegetables.

6 Immaculate conception was a very clean idea.

5 Philippines is a book in the Bible.

4 Unleveled bread makes messy sandwiches.

3 Jesus died in the cavalry.

2 The Word of God shouldn't be touched because it's "sharp" (Hebrews 4:12).

1 God listens to so many people you have to pray and be fast.

Where is drag racing mentioned in the Bible?

Answer

Paul was "beaten with rods" three times and dragged in the streets.

(2 Corinthians 11:25, KJV)

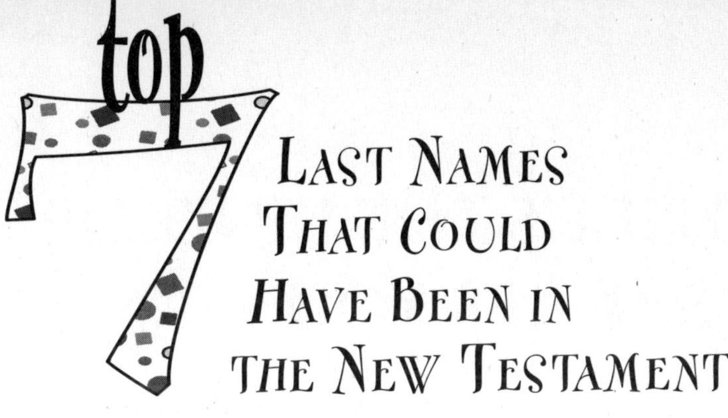

Top 7 Last Names That Could Have Been in the New Testament

7 Mark *Down*

6 Luke *Warm*

5 Theophilus *Mess*

4 Barnabus *Stop*

3 Justus *Iam*

2 Phoebe *Sting*

1 Titus *Over*

HONORABLE MENTION: Pilate *Here* and Rhoda *Construction*

HERE'S THE KIND OF BANKER YOU WANT

"I am looking for what may be credited to your account."

(Philippians 4:17)

PAUL'S ENDORSEMENT IN THE GOVERNOR'S RACE

"For I have no man likeminded, who will naturally care for your state."

(Philippians 2:20, KJV)

Christian Pick-Up Lines

7 Just looking at you makes me feel all ecumenical!

6 Didn't we meet at Bible study?

5 Paul said greet one another with a holy kiss, but I'll settle for just a hug.

4 Has God told you yet we're made for each other?

3 Will you pray for me? . . . You just might get me.

2 Do you believe in predestination?

1 Kiss me if I'm wrong, but isn't your name Methuselah?

EVIDENCE THAT ONE OF PAUL'S MISSIONARY JOURNEYS TOOK HIM TO THE UNITED STATES

"I have learned, in whatsoever state I am, therewith to be content."

(Philippians 4:11, KJV)

NEW EVANGELISM METHODS—4

WASHROOM WITNESSING—Write your message on toilet roll holders or on the toilet paper to be used next time a person comes in (the wall would be an acceptable substitute). The person will give your message his or her full attention!

Good Things About Hell

7 You get to hear all those funny freezing-over jokes.

6 There's a subtle blend of sulfur and brimstone in the air.

5 No one notices your flaming athlete's foot.

4 There are no dead worms.

3 Those lava baths really make your skin tingle.

2 Fish from the lake of fire are already cooked.

1 None of those goody-two shoes Christians are there.

INSTRUCTIONS FOR YOUR LOCAL HONDA DEALER

"You must teach what is in accord."

(Titus 2:1)

NOT A GOOD VERSE FOR A TEACHER TO SHARE WITH STUDENTS

"We have much to say about this, but it is hard to explain because you are slow to learn."

(Hebrews 5:11)

THE LIFE VERSE OF AN EXPEDITER

"The Lord willing, we will go on now to other things."

(Hebrews 6:3, TLB)

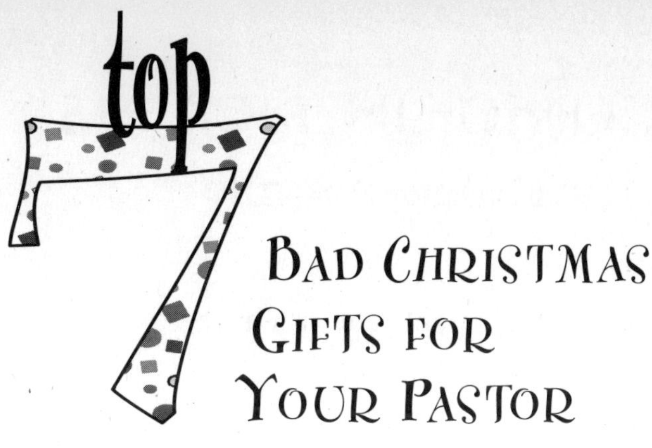

Top 7 Bad Christmas Gifts for Your Pastor

7 Frankincense aftershave

6 St. Peter key chain

5 Golf club covers with the twelve disciples' faces on them

4 The Damascus Road Night-Light (it'll blind ya)

3 A bobbing-head statue of the apostle Paul for the back of the car

2 A millennial prophecy chart

1 Judas Iscariot "Soap on a Rope"

LACONIC LIMERICK #15

Revelation 3:14–22

God will give the churches their due.
Judgment will fall on some too.
If they stay true to form,
Laodicea's lukewarm.
Watch out, here comes a spew!

How do we know that men will get to heaven thirty minutes before women?

Answer

Revelation 8:1 says there will be silence in heaven for about a half-hour.

Ecclesiastical Guffaws

Why do we say "amen" instead of "awomen"?

Answer

Because we sing "hymns," not "hers."

Ways to Tell If Your Pastor Is a Russian Spy

7 You request prayer for a personal problem, and he says he knows all about it.

6 He always wears those medals on his suit.

5 He only reads the red letters in the Bible.

4 He prefers vodka with communion.

3 You saw him talking to his pen.

2 He asks the U.S. government for financial aid.

1 He thinks the apostle Paul was a double agent for the Pharisees.

NEW EVANGELISM METHODS—5

SPAM, SPAM, SPAM . . . EVANGELISM—Witness to fifteen thousand people at a time by sending them the same e-mail message. You can send it to the same people for a month. And it's easy—only a few mouse clicks away.

Top 7 Hoped-for Tithe Deductions

7 Wardrobe replacement credit for wear and tear on all church attire

6 Home mortgage payment if a minimum of two church-related fellowships are hosted in any given month

5 3/4 cent credit for each grueling mile to and from all church activities, including church softball, bingo, and any rummage sales held at or by a church

4 Twenty percent credit for all materials purchased at a Christian bookstore

3 Five hundred dollars for perfect Sunday attendance (a deduction to be proud of)

2 Additional five hundred dollars for perfect attendance *and* choir participation (another proud moment)

1 Another five hundred dollars for perfect attendance and on-key choir participation (almost impossible)

NEW EVANGELISM METHODS—6

LITTERBUG EVANGELISM—Write your message on napkins, bottle labels, etc.; then litter them around the town. It's a great way to reach trash collectors and environmentalists, not to mention the curious and civic-minded. You really will be "spreading the Word"!

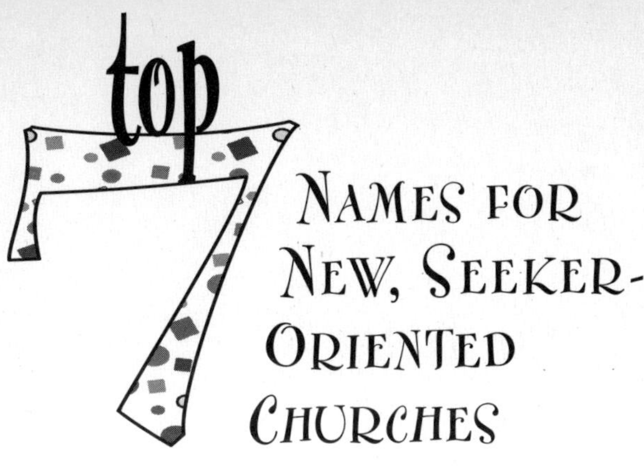

Names for New, Seeker-Oriented Churches

7 It's Happenin' Here Congregation

6 Hip Hop Community Church

5 Inter-non-pan-denominational Fellowship

4 First Church of Love

3 Empathy United Assembly

2 Graceland

1 Saint Good-Enough Chapel

BONUS: Tolerance Tabernacle

BONUS: Have It Your Way House,
with Drive Thru

Top 7 Church Nevers

7 Never base a sermon on an episode of *The Simpsons*.

6 Never ask an usher to break a twenty.

5 Never do a cannonball in the baptismal tank.

4 Never hold a church business meeting on Super Bowl Sunday.

3 Never tell the pastor, "We love your church and might even come back next Easter."

2 During youth group activities, never bungee jump off the church steeple or play chicken with the church buses.

1 After a soloist of impressive size sings "Love Lifted Me," don't follow with the hymn "It Took a Miracle."

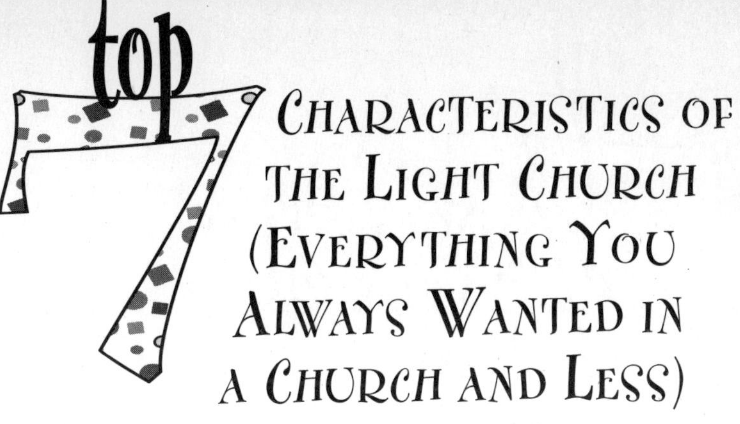

Top 7 Characteristics of the Light Church (Everything You Always Wanted in a Church and Less)

7 Guaranteed thirty-minute sermon or your next one's free!

6 Your choice of only eight commandments

5 Only happy hymns and choruses

4 Fewer commitments

3 No messages on subjects that hit too close to home

2 Reclining pews with pillow pads and headrests

1 Offering followed by a complimentary beverage and after-service mint

Books That Every Pastor Needs

7 *Church Etiquette* by Barney

6 *The Polka in Contemporary Worship*

5 *Martial Arts for the Preschool Sunday School Teacher*

4 *Lifesaving Techniques for Baptismal Accidents*

3 *Health Department Regulations for Church Refrigerators*

2 Dr. Seuss's *One Trib, Two Trib, Post Trib, Mid Trib*

1 *Hairstyles of the Hari Krishna*

Things to Do During a Dull Sermon

7 See how many words you can find in "premillenialism"

6 Send in a prayer-request card for the man next to you with the hair-loss problem

5 Figure out the statistical probability of all the junior highers listening to the sermon at the same time

4 Find a biblical basis for having an ushering staff (perfecting of the saints, maybe?)

3 Draw a picture of the speaker in full "Elvis" gear and present it to him or her after the service

2 Look for back-masking in the hymns sung earlier in the service

1 Listen! Remember, God even used a donkey to speak for him

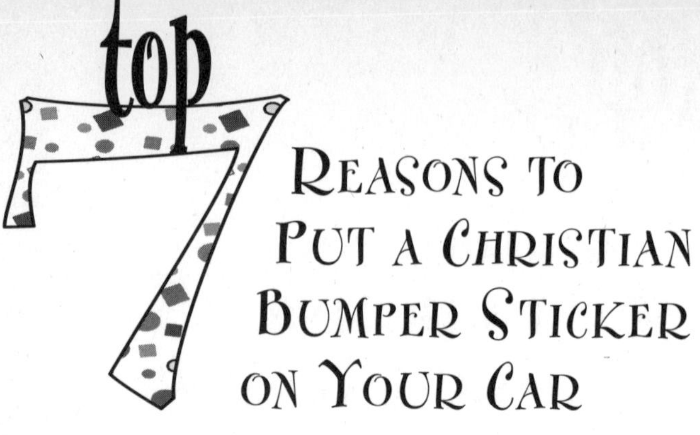

Top 7 Reasons to Put a Christian Bumper Sticker on Your Car

7 Strategic placement of Christian bumper stickers can cause even boxy cars to be more aerodynamic.

6 Many stickers can mask police radar.

5 They're great for covering up those old "Don't Blame Me, I Voted for [fill-in-the-blank]" stickers.

4 Revolutionary adhesion qualities can hold any rusted bumper together.

3 Studies have shown that new color schemes tend to calm the angry motorists behind you.

2 Cars with Christian bumper stickers have fewer accidents than other vehicles.

1 Depending on how you drive, they can be great discussion starters.

Top 7 Things Not to Say During Church

7 "Didn't we already sing that verse?"

6 "I sure hope this check doesn't bounce!"

5 "I have to go to the bathroom."

4 "He forgot the altar call!"

3 "Is there change in there for a twenty?"

2 "I wonder if the roast is burning . . ."

1 "Is this pew saved? (Think about it!)"

NEW EVANGELISM METHODS—7

THE GOSPEL BLIMP—Rent a blimp, then bombard a house, park, town, etc., with tracts, Scripture portions, whatever. For added effect, paint the blimp using your evandalism spray paint.

(Credit to Joe Bayly)

Top 7 Signs Your Church Is in Trouble

7 Your worship service is featured on *America's Funniest Videos*.

6 The Christian education director's nickname is "Scar."

5 The nursery workers have joined the Teamsters Union.

4 A youth group from Appalachia takes a mission trip to repair your facility.

3 The library's most popular book was last checked out in 1979.

2 The average age in the young marrieds class is forty-seven.

1 Last week, the pastor called a "staph" meeting.

Christian Party Games

7 Battle Ark—"Hey, you sunk my battle ark!"

6 Pin the Tail on Baalam's Donkey

5 The Tower of Scrabble (a language game)

4 Kick the Cain and Abel (for those with energy)

3 Spin the Bible

2 Win, Lose, or Purgatory (the TV hit)

1 The Game of Life after Death

Handy Ideas for Christians in the New Millennium

7 Y2K Rummage Sale—great deals on flashlights, battery-powered radios, water containers, and generators

6 Antichrist Early Warning System—if he's close, a light flashes, a bell rings, and the unit vibrates

5 Replacement dust jackets for books that predicted the end of the world

4 Guilt Ray—when aimed at those who profited off the Y2K scare, they feel guilty and give their profits to charity

3 Potluck month—featuring yummy freeze-dried backpacking rations

2 Y2K compliant lawyers—to sue the noncompliant lawyers who first represented us

1 Dictionary 2000—so we can learn what the definition of "is" is

HYMNS FOR VARIOUS OCCUPATIONS

The Dentist's Hymn:
"Crown Him with Many Crowns"

The Meteorologist's Hymn:
"There Shall Be Showers of Blessing"

The Contractor's Hymn:
"The Church's One Foundation"

The Tailor's Hymn: "Holy, Holy, Holy"

The Pro Golfer's Hymn:
"There Is a Green Hill Far Away"

The Politician's Hymn:
"Standing on the Promises"

The Optometrist's Hymn:
"Open Mine Eyes That I Might See"

The IRS Worker's Hymn: "All to Thee"

The Gossip Columnist's Hymn: "Pass It On"

The Electrician's Hymn: "Send the Light"

The Salesperson's Hymn: "Sweet By and By"

Top 7 Signs That Your Church Fund-Raising Campaign Is in Trouble

7 Your consultant's first name is "Fingers."

6 Half of the letters were returned, stamped "addressee unknown."

5 The pledge cards were printed on tissue paper.

4 You have been receiving fast-food coupons in the offering plate.

3 Commitment Sunday falls during spring break.

2 The chairperson recommends recycling aluminum cans as a major funding source.

1 Most members think "Faith Promise" is a church secretary.

IF YOU MUST SPEED ON THE HIGHWAY, SING THESE HYMNS LOUDLY:

at 45 mph—"God Will Take Care of Me"

at 55 mph—"Guide Me, O Thou Great Jehovah"

at 65 mph—"Nearer My God to Thee"

at 75 mph—"Nearer Still Nearer"

at 85 mph—"This World Is Not My Home"

at 95 mph—"Lord, I'm Coming Home"

at 100 mph—"Precious Memories"

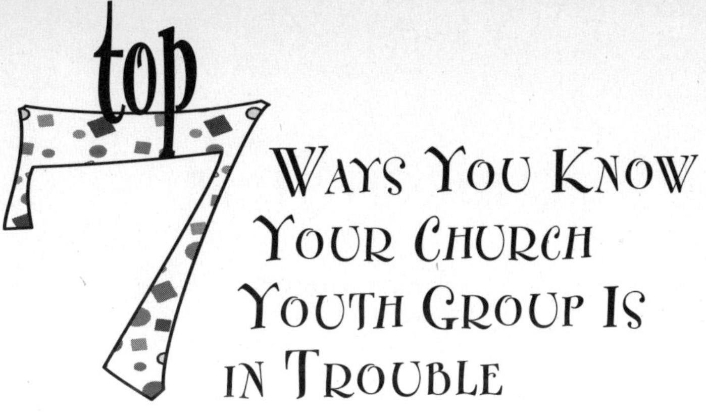

Top 7 Ways You Know Your Church Youth Group Is in Trouble

7 You can't break into small groups because you're already a small group.

6 The elders insist on installing a metal detector at the door of the youth lounge.

5 The grand jury has offered immunity to your most popular adult volunteer.

4 The church has given the youth director an unlisted number.

3 On next year's church budget, the youth ministry falls under the miscellaneous category.

2 The youth director's door is always open because someone has stolen it.

1 The name of the group is Keen Teens.

CHURCH STAFF

Ian Charge	senior pastor
Sandy Scule	director of Christian education
Mary Jung	wedding coordinator
Rich Mann	treasurer
Obie Kynde	visitation chair
Ron D. Block	sports ministry director
Marty Grah	social chair
Jay L. Free	prison ministries coordinator
Mack Romei	craft fair director
Warren Owt	junior high ministry volunteer
Ben Hye	support group facilitator
Sally Forthe	director of evangelism
Ann Onymous	church secretary

Top 7 Indications That Your Bible Study/Sunday School Class Is in Trouble

7 When asked for favorite verses, quotes come from Ben Franklin, the Koran, and the Book of Hesitations.

6 Half of the class shows up just in time for refreshments.

5 Everyone is pretty sure that Jerry and Ray Aboam were brothers (Jeroboam and Rehoboam; see 1 Kings 11:26–14:31).

3 Your meeting room is next door to the junior high class.

2 Everyone wants to discuss the latest *X-Files* episode.

1 All that snoring!

top 7 Signs That Your Sermon's in Trouble

7 You realize that you inadvertently picked up your grocery shopping list instead of your notes.

6 Your guest missionary uses your text and main points in her testimony.

5 The dysfunctional family from your former church hundreds of miles away that you had planned to use as an important illustration is visiting today.

4 After venturing out from behind the pulpit, you realize that your fly is open.

3 The PA is picking up a cellular phone call.

2 The congregation answers your rhetorical questions aloud with the wrong answers.

1 You pound the pulpit and it breaks.

7 Make some cherubim or seraphim in the snow.

6 Groom your Chia tower of Babel.

5 Practice spiritual snowball warfare.

4 Iron your genuine holy lands prayer towels.

3 Build a snow apostle in the front yard.

2 Make an ice sculpture of the Last Supper.

1 Dust off that Amy Grant Christmas album and see if your turntable still works.

Top 7 Pet Peeves of a Televangelist

7 A bad hair day

6 Cuts in Social Security benefits

5 *Inside Edition* and *60 Minutes*

4 Being dropped by the station for *Charlie's Angels* reruns

3 The wife's Mary Kay bill

2 The IRS

1 People who say that halitosis, not the Holy Spirit, made them fall

Things Never Heard in Church

7 "Hey, it's my turn to sit in the front pew!"

6 "Personally, I find witnessing much more enjoyable than golf."

5 "I've decided to give our church the five hundred dollars a month that I used to give to televangelists."

4 "I volunteer to be the permanent teacher for the junior high Sunday school class."

3 "I love it when we sing songs that I've never heard before."

2 "Pastor, we'd like to send you to this Bible seminar in the Bahamas."

1 "Nothing inspires me and strengthens my commitment like our annual stewardship campaign."

Top 7 Excuses for Missing a Meeting

7 "No one told me about it."

6 "The weather was too bad."

5 "The weather was too good."

4 "My computer was down."

3 "I got stopped by a train" or, "The traffic was horrible."

2 "I was so busy."

1 "I forgot."

Makeovers Being Explored by Satan

7 Learning to play the guitar and lip-sync Spice Girls hits

6 Has traded red suit and pitchfork for a Hawaiian shirt and a baseball cap

5 Using phrases like "okey dokie" and "swell"

4 Toning up with the help of *Sweating to the Oldies* and *Buns of Steel*

3 Has hired publicist used by Marilyn Manson and Dr. Jack Kevorkian

2 Is spreading rumors that he's not all bad, just mostly bad

1 Is dropping "Prince of Darkness" moniker for the hipper "Brimstone Ombudsman"

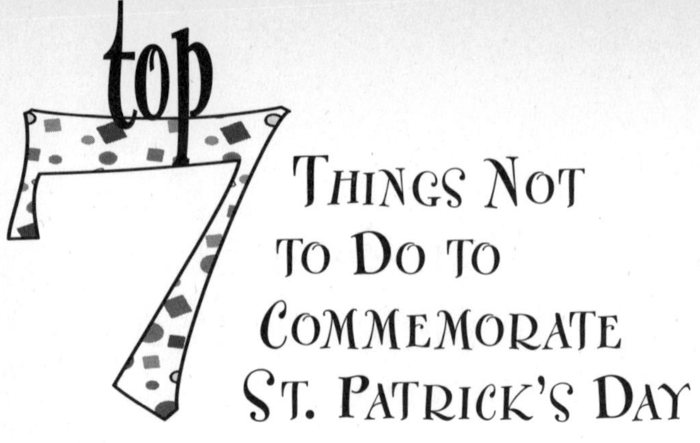

Top 7 Things Not to Do to Commemorate St. Patrick's Day

7 For communion, use green wafers and shamrock shakes

6 Eat corned beef and cabbage before going door-to-door witnessing

5 Sing "Danny Boy" as a praise song

4 Buy your pastor a six-pack of green root beer

3 Become green with envy over your neighbor's pot of gold

2 Throw a party for your guardian leprechaun

1 Tell Irish converts that the Lord's name is Jesus O'Christ

Rejected Church Promotions

7 Change-the-Oil-in-the-Church-Bus Sunday (be sure to wear grubbies)

6 Musical Chairs Sunday (the congregation rotates chairs during each special music number)

5 Grape-Juice-and-Cheese-Whiz Sunday

4 No-Offerings-Will-Be-Taken Sunday

3 Kids-Eat-Free-Potluck Sunday

2 Do-It-Yourself-Worship Sunday

1 Bring-a-Friend-Take-Home-a-Tomato Sunday

top 7 Signs That Your Pastor Is a Little Loopy

7 Insists that each sermon be introduced with smoke, laser lights, and dancing girls

6 Bathes in the baptismal before the service

5 Frequently quotes Bob the Tomato and Larry the Cucumber in sermons

4 Mandates that the last person served should eat all the remaining communion bread

3 Hosts a Web page for Lava Lamp enthusiasts

2 Has a favorite pastime of watching Jim and Tammy reruns

1 Preaches while wearing golf shoes

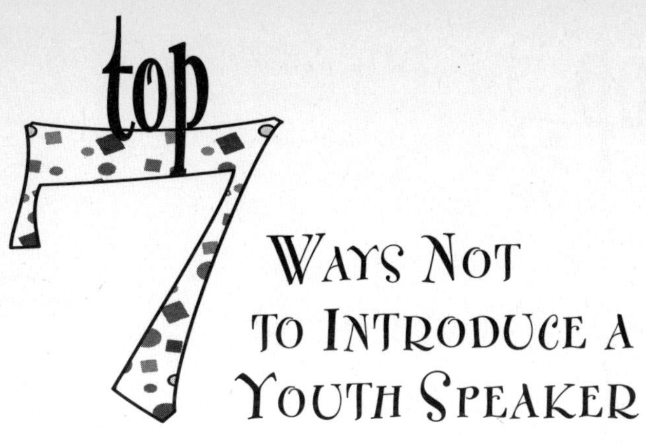

Top 7 Ways Not to Introduce a Youth Speaker

7 A real expert on young people

6 A real groovy dude or dudette

5 A person who, as a child, racked up six perfect-attendance stars in Sunday school

4 The husband of one wife or the wife of one husband

3 A person who's memorized the entire Book of Haggai

2 A person who didn't "inhale"

1 The next Bob Jones

New Church Denominations

7 From the Free Methodists comes Methodists with a Slight Surcharge

6 Star Trek, the Next Denomination

5 Drive-Thru Apostolic

4 The Home Shopping Denomination, now on satellite

3 Temples of the Golden Rule ("Where you give the gold and the elders make the rules")

2 Our Lady of Saint Corningware (big on church dinners)

1 The Assembly of Bapticostal-neo-denom-pseudo-metho-lutheric-post-optional Tribulationists

top 7 Reasons to Wait a Long Time to Get Married

7 You'll have fewer in-law problems—they'll either be "with the Lord" or close to it!

6 You can share Geritol together.

5 He'll have outgrown the sports-car phase.

4 She'll have tired of shopping for the latest fashions.

3 You won't have to worry about your spouse getting fat or bald—he or she will be that way already.

2 Because friends are older, they'll have more money for better wedding gifts.

1 If you wait long enough, you might get to hang out with Paul in the singles-only section in heaven.

Christian Oxymorons

7 *Comfortable pews*—Did you ever try to sleep on one? (Oh, you have, huh?)

6 *Short sermon*—Did you ever try not to sleep through one? (Just kidding.)

5 *Heated baptistry*—Even fundamentalists shout "Glory!" when they hit the water.

4 *Vacation Bible School*—Did you ever teach in VBS? (Vacation for who?)

3 *Exciting deacon meeting*—Come on, it's called a "bored" meeting.

2 *Part-time pastor*—Only if you consider TWELVE hours as half a day.

1 *Modern Gospel*—Jesus Christ: the same yesterday, today, and forever.

Top 7 Signs Your Neighbor Is a Cult Leader

7 Always has a large selection of used firearms at his or her garage sales

6 Has a bumper sticker that reads "Could I Be the Messiah?"

5 Gets jittery when *America's Most Wanted* comes on

4 Has a flashing neon sign in his picture window that reads "Vacancy"

3 Never misses reruns of *The Adams Family* or *Bewitched*

2 Claimed deductions for twelve wives on his income-tax return

1 Was voted most likely to deceive by his or her high school class

Excuses for Missing Church

7 It's your turn for nursery duty.

6 The last check you dropped in the offering plate bounced.

5 It's not Christmas or Easter.

4 Your dog ate your Bible lesson.

3 You overslept and don't know anyone at the second service.

2 They're recruiting deacons again.

1 It's a seeker service, and you're not lost.

Reasons Churches Don't Ask Clown Ministries to Return

7 They force people to smile at 10 A.M. on Sunday.

6 It's difficult to say with a straight face: "The sermon today will be brought to you by Brother Dimples."

5 Those balloon sculptures of the Last Supper just take too long to construct.

4 Clowns wearing blue curly wigs might be confused with the older sisters.

3 Seltzer-water baptism is not recognized by your denomination.

2 Dribble glasses may be used for communion.

1 The ushers don't appreciate all the Monopoly money in the offering plates.

Top 7 Reasons to Play in a Christian Softball League

7 Motivation to pray more for a resurrected body

6 The mercy rule

5 The chance to see if the pastor really did get that athletic scholarship to seminary

4 The warm fuzzy feeling on Sunday morning after playing a doubleheader till 11:30 on Saturday night

3 The possibility of hearing an elder speak in a very peculiar tongue that you won't hear in church

2 The possibility of participating in a healing service

1 Assurance of being brought home on a sacrifice

New Books for Pastors and Churches

7 *Lite Worship*—"Feels Great, Less Filling"

6 *Clogging and Other Creative Worship Options*

5 *The One-Minute Sermon*

4 *Church Growth through Proselytizing*

3 *Let's Build a Baptistry*

2 *Preach and Lose Weight*

1 *Bibles, Bullets, and Beauties: Proof Texts for Every Occasion*

Top 7 Slogans Seen on Church Marquees

7 "Join our sit-in demonstration every Sunday."

6 "Come in and pray today—beat the Christmas rush."

5 "Keep off the grass. This means thou."

4 "Last chance to pray before entering the freeway."

3 "All new sermons—no reruns."

2 "God so loved the world that he didn't send a committee."

1 "K-Mart isn't the only saving place."

New Books on Spiritual Growth

7 *Discipling for Dummies*

6 *How to Fast Between Meals*

5 *Deferred Tithing*

4 *Living Simply for Fun and Profit (and Prophet)*

3 *Betcha Can't Quit Gambling*

2 *101 New Clichés*

1 *Sacrifice Made Easy*

STAFF DESCRIPTIONS

Senior Pastor

Leaps tall buildings in a single bound
Is more powerful than a locomotive
Is faster than a speeding bullet
Walks on water
Gives policy to God

Associate Pastor

Leaps short buildings in a single bound
Is more powerful than a switch engine
Is just as fast as a speeding bullet
Walks on water if sea is calm
Talks with God

Adult Ministries Director

Leaps short buildings with a running start and favorable winds
Is almost as powerful as a switch engine
Is faster than a speeding BB
Walks on water in an indoor swimming pool
Talks with God if special request is approved

Christian Education Director

Barely clears a Quonset hut
Loses tug of war with locomotive
Can fire a speeding bullet
Swims well
Is occasionally addressed by God

Youth Director

Makes high marks on the walls
when trying to leap tall buildings
Is run over by locomotives
Can sometimes handle a gun without
inflicting self-injury
Frequently uses water fountain
Talks to animals

Intern

Runs into buildings
Recognizes locomotives two out of three times
Is not issued ammunition
Can stay afloat with a life jacket
Talks to walls

Volunteer

Falls over doorstep when trying to enter building
Says "look at the choo-choo"
Is given only a water pistol
Mumbles to himself/herself

Church Secretary

Lifts buildings and walks under them
Kicks locomotives off the tracks
Catches speeding bullets in his/her teeth and eats them
Freezes water with a single glance
He/she is god

Top 7 Things to Do on Really Hot Days

7 Play in your "Jonah's Great Fish" lawn sprinkler

6 Have a group baptism at your favorite beach

5 Take that missions trip to Alaska

4 Use the heat in your witnessing spiel, for example, "If you think *this* is hot . . ."

3 Be like Job and shave your head

2 Repent for what you said last January when the temperature was 25 below.

1 Build your faith—practice walking on water (anyone can do it in January)

Top 7 Lists We're Still Working On

7 The Top 7 Denominations on God's Most-Favored List

6 The Top 7 Wives of Solomon

5 The Top 7 Really Good Reasons to Pay Caesar More

4 The Top 7 Works That Will Get a Person into Heaven

3 The Top 7 Scientific Discoveries That Support Evolution

2 The Top 7 Good Things Satan Has Done

1 The Top 7 *Christianity Today* Swimsuit Issues